"Dell's story is the stuff high-tech le

"Computer maker Dell is showing the world how to run a business in the cyberage." —*Business Week*

"There is tumult in the personal computer industry and it is due largely to one man: Michael Dell. Competitors would love to match its ability to quickly accept orders, build the PCs, then move them to buyers. But Dell is setting the standard." —*USA Today*

"The thing that sets Dell apart is its ability to do exactly what the competition tends to believe cannot be done. . . . It's scary to think where [Michael Dell's] going to be in ten years—he's going to be a powerhouse in the computer industry after Lou Gerstner's successor's successor retires." —*Fortune*

"In the past three years, Dell has been on a jihad to make its manufacturing and assembly process as fast and fine-tuned as a Mercedes. The result: Dell is now one of high-tech's best growth engines." —*Business Week*

"Dell is to the computer industry what Dominos is to pizza delivery: fast, dependable, and ubiquitous." —*Time*

"The do-it-the-customer's way mantra has created for Dell the tightest—and most envied—relationship with buyers in the PC business." —*Business Week*

"Dell is famous in the business for its strict inventory controls, and is envied for its margins. . . . This is one smart operation."
—*San Jose Mercury News*

Direct from

Direct from

Strategies That Revolutionized an Industry

MICHAEL DELL
with Catherine Fredman

HarperBusiness
An Imprint of HarperCollinsPublishers

All net proceeds from *Direct From Dell* will be contributed to the Dell Foundation, a charitable organization unaffiliated with the Dell family that is dedicated to serving the needs of children.

Dell, Dimension, Latitude, OptiPlex, Inspiron, and PowerEdge are registered trademarks, and Premier Pages and DellPlus are service marks of Dell Computer Corporation. The Dell logo is property of Dell Computer Corporation and used with the permission of Dell Computer Corporation.

Other trademarks and tradenames used in this book refer either to the entities claiming the marks and names, or to their products. Dell disclaims proprietary interest in the marks and names of others.

Fast Cycle Segmentation chart on page 75 reprinted by permission of *Harvard Business Review*. Copyright 1998 by the President and Fellows of Harvard College.

A hardcover edition of this book was published by HarperBusiness, an imprint of HarperCollins Publishers, in 1999.

DIRECT FROM DELL. Copyright © 1999 by Michael Dell. All rights reserved. Printed in the United States of America. No part of this book may be used or reproduced in any manner whatsoever without written permission except in the case of brief quotations embodied in critical articles and reviews. For information address HarperCollins Publishers Inc., 10 East 53rd Street, New York, NY 10022.

HarperCollins books may be purchased for educational, business, or sales promotional use. For information please write: Special Markets Department, HarperCollins Publishers Inc., 10 East 53rd Street, New York, NY 10022.

First paperback edition published 2000.

Designed by Christine Weathersbee

The Library of Congress has catalogued the hardcover edition as follows:

Dell, Michael, 1965–
   Direct from Dell : strategies that revolutionized an industry / Michael Dell with Catherine Fredman.
     p. cm.
   Includes index.
   ISBN 0-88730-914-3
   1. Dell Computer Corp.—History. 2. Computer industry—United States—History. I. Fredman, Catherine. II. Title.
   HD9696.2.U64D45 1999
   338.7'6213916'0973—dc21   98-53437

ISBN 0-88730-915-1 (pbk.)

00 01 02 03 04 ❖/RRD 10 9 8 7 6 5 4 3 2 1

CONTENTS

Contents

This book is dedicated with love to my family:
Susan, Kira, Alexa, Zachary, and Juliette

ACKNOWLEDGMENTS

FIRST, I AM GRATEFUL TO MY FRIENDS whose support and encouragement have been steadfast, through good times and bad. Without them, the rise of Dell, as described in this book, would have been impossible.

Our customers have been a constant source of inspiration and learning; they have provided us with the ideas and feedback that are the basis of our success.

My parents instilled a curiosity and drive that continues to serve me well. I thank them for understanding a son who followed an unusual path.

The men and women of Dell Computer Corporation continue to prove that the innovation and commitment of its people are what takes any good company and makes it great. I especially want to thank my colleagues on the executive team, who make the adventure of running our company fun on a daily basis, and who continue to shape my thinking.

Three women have offered close collaboration on this project:

Catherine Fredman, my creative partner, who through her research and probing questions brought this project to life and helped turn my ideas into something understandable on paper; my editor, Laureen "You have to do this Book!" Rowland, who provided invaluable help and mobilized the full resources of HarperCollins; and Michele Moore of Dell, who played an indispensable role on this project, and on so many others over the years.

Last but not least, I would like to thank my wonderful wife, Susan, for her never-ending support, encouragement, love, and tremendously positive attitude. I could not ask for better partner in life!

—*Michael Dell*
Round Rock, Texas
February 1999

TIMELINE

1980

In a harbinger of what would come, Michael Dell purchases his first computer—an Apple II—and promptly takes it apart to understand how it was designed and made.

1983

Declaring he ultimately wanted to beat IBM, the young Dell conducts a lucrative business out of his dormitory room at the University of Texas, selling upgraded PCs and add-on components.

1984

With $1,000 in startup capital, Michael registers his business as Dell Computer Corporation, doing business as PC's Limited, and leaves school in May of that year. The company becomes the first in the industry to sell custom-built computers directly to end-users, bypassing the dominant system of using computer resellers to sell mass-produced computers.

1986

Dell unveils the industry's fastest-performing computer, a 12 MHz, 286-based system, at the Spring Comdex national computer tradeshow. The system quickly garners rave reviews from the technology press.

The company also pioneers the industry's first thirty-day money back guarantee, which becomes the cornerstone of Dell's commitment to expand its service offerings and offer superior customer satisfaction, and offers the industry's first onsite service program.

1987

In a bold move for the fledgling operation, Dell establishes its first international subsidiary in the United Kingdom. Eleven more international operations would open over the course of the next four years.

1988

Dell raises $30 million in its initial public offering, bringing the market capitalization of the company, begun with $1,000 in capital, to $85 million.

1989

The fast-growing company experiences its first major stumbles: It accumulates excess inventory of memory components, which results in write-downs, and cancels an overambitious product development program code-named "Olympic."

1990

Dell becomes the first computer company to jump into the burgeoning market for computers sold through consumer retail stores such as CompUSA and Best Buy. The company later becomes the first company to exit this segment as well, after determining the retail-store model did not meet its financial objectives.

1991

Converting its entire product line to the highest-performing Intel 486 microprocessors, Dell demonstrates its commitment to rapidly delivering the latest technology to its customers.

1992

Dell achieves slightly more than $2 billion in sales for the fiscal year ended January 1993, which represents a remarkable 127 percent increase.

1993

Suffering from the pains of extremely rapid growth, Dell cancels a secondary offering and posts its only quarterly loss resulting from a temporary withdrawal from the notebook market, its exit from retail stores, and a restructuring of European operations.

"Liquidity, profitability, and growth" become a company mantra, signifying its shift from a focus on growth alone to more balanced priorities. *Upside* magazine gives Michael Dell the dubious distinction of "Turnaround CEO of the Year."

1994

Following a hiatus from major participation in the market for notebook computers, Dell launches its new Latitude notebook line with record-breaking battery life.

Following the earlier launch of Dell Japan, Dell opens its first operations in the Asia-Pacific region, which has become the fastest-growing international startup in the company's history.

1996

Dell challenges the traditional market for premium-priced servers based on proprietary technology with its introduction of its PowerEdge server line. In less than two years, PowerEdge vaults Dell from the tenth position in market share to the third largest server vendor in the world.

The company's quiet bid to sell custom-built computers over the Internet quickly becomes a public revolution when the company announces that sales over *www.dell.com* have exceeded $1 million per day. During the same year, Dell introduces its first custom-made web links for customers. Called "Premier Pages," the links allow customers to tap directly into the company's own service and support databases.

1998

Dell solidifies its Internet leadership when it tops $12 million per day over the Internet, expands its Premier Page program to more than nine thousand customers and establishes web-based connections with its suppliers to speed the flow of inventory and quality information.

Dell opens an integrated sales, manufacturing, and support center in China.

1999

Dell becomes the number one PC company in the United States, the largest worldwide market for personal computers. To accomodate its growth, Dell opens new manufacturing facilities in Nashville, Tennessee and Eldorado do Sul, Brazil.

Sales over *www.dell.com* top $35 million per day.

FOREWORD

OUR COMPANY BEGAN THE DECADE OF THE 1990S as the 25th-ranked computer company in the world, behind brands that you've probably forgotten or never even heard of—companies like Mitac, Tandon, and Commodore. We operated in barely a handful of international locations. And because computers were then sold only through resellers, Dell's direct business model was viewed as an alternative and limited way of doing business.

Today, 17 out of the top 25 computer companies in 1990 no longer exist. But Dell is the number-one ranked company in the U.S. and the second-largest company, globally. We operate in 170 countries around the world. And "direct" is widely recognized as the preferred way of doing business. But the recognition of direct as the best way to do business is not limited to the computer industry. CEOs from industries as diverse as banking, automotive, and logistics pharmaceuticals have told me their most important strategic challenge is to make their company more direct. Why? The benefits are clear: customers order and receive products or services directly from the manufacturer, made to their exact specifications, and firms operate at maximum efficiency by not producing a product until they know it is sold.

It is true that our rise to prominence has been largely due to our dedicated focus on our direct-to-the-customer way of doing business, and to the management principles I've discussed in this book. But it is also true that our success—and the failure of many once-promising computer companies—reflects the incredibly rapid pace of change in the technology industry, and the danger that can come from not being quick enough to recognize, and respond to, new competitive forces.

The Internet has brought the pace of change that we've experienced in the technology industry to all industries, and with much greater intensity. Consider this simple example. Five years ago, if a group of 100 college-age students were asked whether they ever bought a book or CD online, the answer would likely be zero. Ask the same group that question today, and those who say yes would probably be close to 100. Now ask this sample group if they would consider buying a car online today.

Roughly 50 percent would say yes. How many will say yes in five years? I'm willing to bet the number will approach 95 percent.

The point is that the deployment of the Internet has just begun. The adoption of the Internet continues at a rapid pace and in this new connected environment, the continued success of our company—or yours—is by no means assured.

The Internet changes the fundamental nature of competition. As new ways of bundling products and services online emerge, your competition goes beyond established competitors to include companies you've not heard of yet, in addition to new innovations, ideas or ways of improving existing processes or products.

This is not a new phenomenon. Wal-Mart's fast rise in the late 1980s took the established retail industry by surprise, similar to how Nucor and other "mini-mills" shook the steel industry earlier in that decade. These companies created new business models outside the norm of traditional competition and in so doing, created new sources of customer value and profit.

The difference today is that the Internet dramatically increases the speed at which new businesses emerge and become established.

One reason is that the Internet changes the nature of capital formation, in that initial public stock offerings more closely resemble an invitation to invest in a venture capital fund, than an opportunity to invest in established company fundamentals. This gives emerging companies huge amounts of capital with which to experiment, whether it be through web-based business models or through acquisitions.

Another reason is that the Internet puts control firmly in the hands of the buyer, not the seller, as geography and physical location become largely irrelevant to price and product selection. Businesses that had an advantage because they sold things in a geographic area where people had limited information and couldn't travel to buy another brand are in real trouble.

I'm often asked to speak about Dell's early adoption of the Internet, and the lessons we have learned that can be applied to other businesses.

Most of our learning has been experiential, through trial and error. And as I've described in this book, that is one of the greatest beauties of the Internet: the immediacy of customer reaction online makes experimenting relatively easy and lower cost.

Our direct business model also gives us a natural advantage as business moves online: because we have always had a direct relationship with our customers, we don't have to grapple with issues that arise from alienating resellers or distributors in order to establish direct Internet connections.

Even so, the lessons we have learned—what I call the "rules for Internet revolutionaries"—are, I believe, applicable in any company, in any industry.

First, velocity, or the compression of time and distance backward into the supply chain and forward to the customer, will be the ultimate source of competitive advantage. Use the Internet to lower the cost of developing links between manufacturers and suppliers, and manufacturers and customers. This will make it possible to get products and services faster to market than ever before.

Second, efficiency and execution will be at least as important as products and services. Turn over to outsiders operations that aren't central to your business advantage; this will free capital to invest in activities with higher value to your customers. How easy you make it for customers to buy and receive your products or services, and the economies you are able to provide to them by effectively harnessing the Internet, are just as important to online brand differentiation as what it is you have to sell.

This leads to the third and most important lesson we have learned: the web experience must be better than any experience in the physical world to create truly sustainable customer relationships and loyalty. Those companies for which the quality of experience has never been a part of the customer attraction—companies like discount drugstores and auto parts stores—will be particularly vulnerable to the onslaught of Internet ventures where shopping not only offers a rich and low-cost selection, but also convenience and personalized service as well. Experiment with Internet businesses; develop trials to see what customers value when they can access information in ways they never could before.

For Dell, each of these tenets has had their foundation in the lessons of direct. These are the lessons I've described in this book, and they continue to serve us well.

PREFACE

"I've Always Been Fascinated with Eliminating Unnecessary Steps"

WHEN I WAS IN THIRD GRADE, I SENT away for a high school diploma.

I had seen the advertisement in the back of a magazine: "Earn your high school diploma by passing one simple test," it said. It's not like I had anything against school; I liked third grade. And getting a good education had always been really important in my family.

But at that age, I was both impatient and curious. If there was a way to get something done more quickly and easily, I wanted to try it. And trading nine years of school for "one simple test" seemed like a pretty good idea to me.

Early one evening, a woman from the testing company appeared at the door of my family's home in Houston. My mother answered, and the woman politely asked for Mr. Michael Dell. At first, my mother was puzzled. But after asking a few questions, she figured out what was going on.

"He's taking a bath right now, but I'll call him," she said. Much to the woman's surprise, out I came, an eight-year-old, in a red terry-cloth bathrobe.

Both my parents and the woman from the testing company thought I had applied to take the test as a joke. But I was quite serious.

Since an early age, I've been fascinated with the idea of eliminating unnecessary steps. So I guess it's not surprising that I started a company based on eliminating the middleman. Dell sells computers directly to our customers, deals directly with our suppliers, and communicates directly with our people, all without the unnecessary and inefficient presence of intermediaries. We call this "the direct model," and it has taken us, to use a common phrase at Dell Computer Corporation, "direct to the top."

In 1998, we became the number two manufacturer and marketer of personal computers in the world. We grew five times faster than the industry rate. Our stock rose more than 200 percent—the largest share-price gain in the S&P 500 and the NASDAQ 100.

People have often told us that what we wanted to do couldn't be done.

Our success is due, in part, to not just an ability but a willingness to look at things differently. I believe opportunity is part instinct and part immersion—in an industry, a subject, or an area of expertise. Dell is proof that people can learn to recognize and take advantage of opportunities that others are convinced don't exist. You don't have to be a genius, or a visionary, or even a college graduate to think unconventionally. You just need a framework and a dream.

This book is neither my memoir nor a complete history of Dell Computer Corporation. Rather I hope it will be a guide to developing and honing your competitive edge, no matter what industry you're in or what your role is. We happen to have succeeded in the computer industry, but seeing and seizing opportunities are skills that can be applied universally, if you have the curiosity and commitment. And because of the unique way in which Dell was started in my dorm room at the University of Texas, the trajectory of my own development as an entrepreneur and then CEO is inextricably bound to the development of the company.

In these pages, we'll explore what we have come to term our "competitive strategies"—speed to market; superior customer service; a fierce commitment to producing consistently high quality, custom-made computer systems that provide the highest performance and the latest relevant technology to our customers; and an early exploitation of the Internet. In Part One, I describe how these strategies took hold, born of good times and bad, as the company grew and changed and grew some more. In Part Two, you'll see how we've enhanced these strategies. And how, by finding innovative ways to combine technology with the information we glean from our direct relationships with employees, customers, and suppliers, Dell has developed its most critical competitive advantage: becoming a virtually integrated organization.

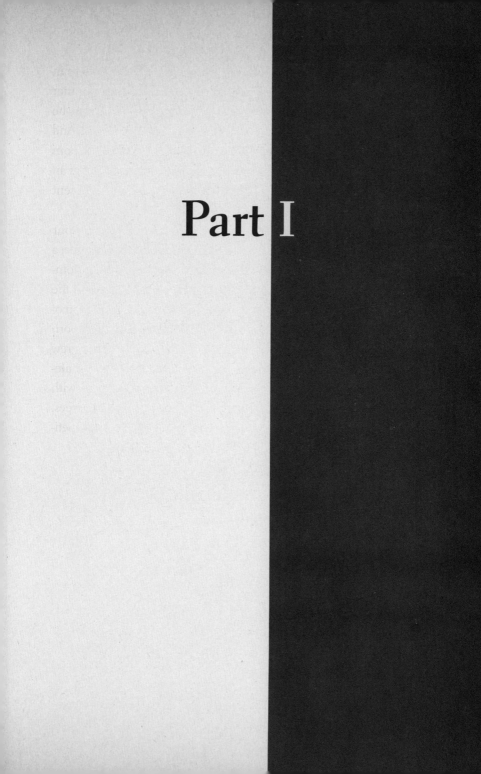

Part I

THE BIRTH OF BEING DIRECT

I **FIRST EXPERIENCED THE POWER—AND**
the rewards—of being direct when I was twelve years old. The
father of my best friend in Houston was a pretty avid stamp collector,
so naturally my friend and I wanted to get into stamp collecting, too.
To fund my interest in stamps, I got a job as a water boy in a Chinese
restaurant two blocks from my house. I started reading stamp jour-
nals just for fun, and soon began noticing that prices were rising.
Before long, my interest in stamps began to shift from the joy of collecting to the idea that there was something here that my mother, a
stockbroker, would have termed "a commercial opportunity."

In our household, you couldn't help being aware of commercial
opportunities. The discussions at our dinner table in the 1970s were
about what the chairman of the Federal Reserve was doing and how
it affected the economy and the inflation rate; the oil crisis; which

companies to invest in, and which stocks to sell and buy. The economy in Houston was booming at the time, and the market for collectibles was quite active. It was obvious to me from what I'd read and heard that the value of stamps was increasing, and being a fairly resourceful kid, I saw this as an opportunity.

My friend and I had already bought stamps at an auction, and since I knew even then that people rarely did something for nothing, I assumed that the auctioneers were making a decent fee. Rather than pay them to buy the stamps, I thought it would be fun to create my own auction. Then I could learn even more about stamps *and* collect a commission in the process.

I was about to embark upon one of my very first business ventures.

First, I got a bunch of people in the neighborhood to consign their stamps to me. Then I advertised "Dell's Stamps" in *Linn's Stamp Journal*, the trade journal of the day. And then I typed, with one finger, a twelve-page catalog (I didn't yet know how to type, nor did I have a computer) and mailed it out.

Much to my surprise, I made $2,000. And I learned an early, powerful lesson about the rewards of eliminating the middleman. I also learned that if you've got a good idea, it pays to do something about it.

SEEING THE PATTERN

A few years later, I saw the chance to seize an even greater opportunity. When I was sixteen, I got a summer job selling newspaper subscriptions to *The Houston Post*. At the time, the newspaper gave its salespeople a list of new phone numbers issued by the telephone company and told us to cold call them. It struck me as a pretty random way of approaching new business.

I soon noticed a pattern, however, based on the feedback I was getting from potential customers during these conversations. There were two kinds of people who almost always bought subscriptions to the *Post*: people who had just married and people who had just moved into new houses or apartments. With this in mind, I wondered, "How could you find all the people who are getting mortgages or getting married?"

After asking around, I discovered that when a couple wanted to get married, they had to go to the county courthouse and get a marriage license. They also had to provide the address to which the license would be sent. In the state of Texas, that information is public. So I hired a couple of my high school buddies and we canvassed the courthouses in the sixteen counties surrounding the Houston area, collecting the names and addresses of the newly (or soon-to-be-newly) married.

Then I found out that certain companies compiled lists of people who had applied for mortgages. These lists were ranked by the size of the mortgage. You could easily identify the people with the largest mortgages and go after those high-potential customers first.* I targeted these people, creating a personalized letter and offering them a subscription to the newspaper.

By this time, summer was over and it was time to go back to high school. As important as school was, I found that it could be very disruptive to a steady income. I had worked hard to create a lucrative system and didn't want to just throw it away, so I handled the bulk of the work during the week after school, and I did the follow-up work on Saturday mornings. The subscriptions came in by the thousands.

One day, my history and economics teacher assigned us a project for which we had to file our tax returns. Based on what I had made selling newspaper subscriptions, my income was about $18,000 that year. At first, my teacher corrected me, assuming I had missed the decimal

---

*This was my first experience with what I would later call "segmenting the market," one of Dell's most significant strategies for success.

place. When she realized I hadn't, she became even more dismayed.

To her surprise, I had made more money that year than she had.

ENTER THE COMPUTER

By then, I had a new hobby: computers. In fact, my interest in computers goes back even further. From the time I was seven, when I purchased my first calculator, I was fascinated by the idea of a machine that could compute things. In junior high school, I was in an advanced math class and had joined a Number Sense Club, whose members did complicated math problems in their heads and competed in math contests. Our coach, a math teacher named Mrs. Darby, installed the first teletype terminal in our junior high school. If you stayed after school, you could play around with it and write programs or input equations and get back answers. It was the most amazing thing I'd ever seen.

I started hanging around at Radio Shack and playing with their computers. And I started saving money to buy my own. At the time, the Apple was easily the most popular personal computer in the United States, and the one with the most software, which was important. The beautiful thing about the Apple II was that it wasn't as complicated as today's computers. Every circuit was on its own unique chip, and you could easily open up the box and figure out how the computer worked. *Byte* magazine regularly described the latest components, and the semiconductor companies published manuals that explained everything you ever wanted to know about their particular chips, so you could pick up a data book to learn what a 74LS07 did and what its inputs and outputs were. I remember reading an article in *Byte* about the first Shugart 5¼-inch floppy disk drive; I thought it was incredibly cool.

I bugged my parents repeatedly to let me buy my own computer and finally, for my fifteenth birthday, they agreed. I didn't have a driver's license yet and was so anxious for my computer to arrive that I made my dad drive me down to the local UPS office to pick it up. Once we pulled back into our driveway, I jumped out of the car, carried the precious cargo to my room, and with great relish, promptly took my new computer apart.

My parents were infuriated.

An Apple cost a lot of money in those days. They thought I had demolished it. I just wanted to see how it worked.

As had happened with stamps, my fascination with computers soon evolved from a hobby into a business opportunity. In 1981, IBM introduced the PC, and I soon switched from Apple to IBM. While the Apple had lots of games, at the time, the IBM PC was more powerful. It had software and programs for business usage, and although I didn't have a lot of business experience, I had enough to know that this PC was going to be *the* choice for business in the future.

Meanwhile, I wanted to learn as much as I could about PCs, so I bought all these other things that would enhance a PC, like more memory, disk drives, bigger monitors, and faster modems. (This was before personal computers had hard drives, so there weren't a great deal of options.) I would enhance a PC the way another guy would soup up a car, and then I would sell it for a profit and do it again. I was soon going to distributors and buying components in bulk to reduce the costs. My mother complained that my room looked like a mechanic's shop.

By some stroke of luck, the 1982 National Computer Conference was held in June at the Astrodome in Houston—four months after I'd gotten my driver's license. (The NCC has since been replaced by Comdex.) I skipped school for much of that week to attend the show; somehow my parents never found out. It was an incredibly eye-opening experience.

I had spent plenty of time in computer stores and had already dealt with component distributors, but I had never been exposed to the computer industry, per se. At the NCC, the whole computer industry was demonstrating the latest prototypes and previewing technology that would soon be coming to market. There, I saw the first 5 megabyte disk drive. (Today, Dell routinely sells personal computers with 37 gigabyte hard drives—more than 7,400 times larger!) I remember going up to the booth of a company called Seagate and asking how much one would cost. I think they cost a few thousand dollars. In response they asked, "Are you an OEM?" I didn't even know what an OEM was.*

I was learning about the computer business.

Eventually I saved up enough money to buy a hard disk drive. I used it to set up a bulletin board system on which I exchanged messages with others interested in computers. And as I compared notes about PCs with other people, I found that there were real anomalies in the sales and markups of these machines.

An IBM PC typically sold in a store for about $3,000. But the components could be purchased for around $600 or $700, and the technology wasn't IBM's. (I knew how much the components cost and who was making them because I was taking the computers apart and upgrading them.) That didn't make a lot of sense to me.

Another thing that didn't make sense was that the people operating the computer stores didn't even know much about PCs. For the most part, they had previously sold stereos or cars, and thought that computers represented the next "big ticket" fad, so they figured, "Why not? We'll sell them, too." Hundreds of computer stores were popping up in Houston. And these dealers would pay about $2,000 for an IBM PC and then sell it for $3,000, making $1,000 profit. They also offered little or no support to the customer. Yet they were making tons of money because people really wanted to buy computers.

---

*"Original equipment manufacturer," a term that's as common in the industry as "profit and loss."

At this point, I was already buying the exact same components that were used in these machines, and I was upgrading my machines and selling them to people I knew. I realized that if I could sell even more of them, I could actually compete with the computer stores—and not just on price but on quality. I could also earn a nice little profit and get all the things your typical high school kid would want.

But beyond that, I thought, "Wow, there's *a lot* of opportunity here."

I was both nervous and excited by the possibilities. My mind was filled with questions: What did I already know that I could use? What did I need to learn? How could I learn it?

But my parents intervened. They had expected me to be a premed major at the University of Texas at Austin, just like my older brother. And so it was. On the day I left for college, I drove off in the white BMW that I had bought with my earnings from selling newspaper subscriptions, with three computers in the backseat of the car.

My mother should have been very suspicious.

THE BIG IDEA TAKES HOLD

I was serious about college. I went to class and I did my work. And I would never advocate that young people today pass up an opportunity for higher education. But my freshman year was boring compared to the idea of starting a business—and not just any business, but one where the opportunities were so readily apparent. Fortunately, the University of Texas at Austin is a very large school. And, well, the benefit of going to a very large school is that nobody really knows what you're doing, so you can drift off and do something else.

Like start a business.

I was probably quite a strange sight to see, walking around campus, books in one hand, a bunch of RAM chips in the other. I would go to class and then after class I would go back to my dorm room to upgrade a few computers. By this time, word of what I was doing had traveled, and businesspeople (as opposed to students)—like attorneys and doctors from the area—were coming by to drop off or pick up their computers.

Because the State of Texas had an open bidding process, any vendor could bid on state contracts. So I applied for a vendor's license. Without the overhead of a computer store, I could sell higher-performance models at a much lower price.

I won a lot of bids.

By November of that year (1983—I was eighteen), my parents had gotten wind of the fact that I wasn't attending classes and my grades were going down. So in a second intervention, they flew up to Austin for a surprise visit. I remember that they called me from the Austin airport to tell me they were there. I had barely enough time to stash all the computers behind the shower curtain in my roommate's bathroom before they walked in. Still, it was obvious that not a lot of studying was going on.

My Dad started. "You've got to stop with this computer stuff and concentrate on school," he said. "Get your priorities straight. What do you want to do with your life?"

"I want to compete with IBM!" I said.

He wasn't amused.

I agreed to stop with the "computer stuff," only to appease my parents. And I tried. I went cold turkey for three weeks. But as well intentioned as I was, I couldn't do it. By December, I knew my fascination with computers wasn't just a hobby or a passing phase. I knew in my heart that I was on to a fabulous business opportunity that I could not let pass me by. Here was a device that so profoundly changed the way people worked—and its cost was coming down. I knew that if you took this tool, previously in the hands of a select few, and made it available to every big business, small business, individual, and student, it could become the most important device of this century.

What I can't say I knew, at age eighteen, was how big the opportunity was. I didn't know exactly how the technology would evolve. And I definitely felt that I was diving into something pretty major without knowing most of the details. There was a lot more that was unknown than known to me then. Like what the barriers for entry into this exploding industry would be. Like how to secure capital, how much I'd need, and how fast the business market would grow.

But I did know one thing. I knew what I wanted to do: build better computers than IBM, offer great value and service to the customer by selling direct, and become number one in the industry.

Besides my parents, I didn't admit that to anyone, because they probably would have thought I was crazy. But to me, the opportunity was clear.

And I felt that this was absolutely the right time to go for it.

THE BIG OPPORTUNITY BECOMES CLEAR

What I saw was a great opportunity to provide computing technology in a much more efficient way. That was the core idea of what became Dell Computer Corporation, and it's one that we've stuck with ever since.

Traditionally, in the computer industry, a manufacturing company built computers, which were then distributed to resellers and dealers who sold them to businesses and individual consumers. In the early days, companies like Apple and IBM sold their products through computer dealers because they needed the leverage to gain nationwide sales. When IBM introduced the original IBM PC, even though IBM had the most sophisticated field sales organization in the world, they chose to sell their PCs the same way. With the biggest players at that time all oriented to the idea of selling through resellers, people believed that the indirect channel was simply the way to go.

But the indirect channel was based on a marriage of the unknowing buyer and the unknowledgeable seller. I knew that marriage could not last. I had grown up with computers. Every paper I wrote in high school had been written on a computer. Computers were already well integrated into my life, and it seemed obvious to me that it was just a matter of time before every business, every school, and every individual started to rely on them. Even in 1984 you could say, "Ten years from now there will be millions and millions of more knowledgeable PC users." What wasn't as clear then was that there could be as many as 1.4 *billion* PCs in use by 2008, as I believe today. But I knew the market would be huge. And I knew, based on my own experience as a user—and my limited experience with customers—that customers would become even more knowledgeable and demanding every year.

I started the business with a simple question: How can we make the process of buying a computer better? The answer was: Sell computers directly to the end customer. Eliminate the reseller's markup and pass those savings on to the customer.

It didn't occur to me that others hadn't figured this out. I thought it was pretty obvious. I'm sure if I had taken the time to ask, plenty of people would have told me that my idea wouldn't work—I've heard that a lot in the fifteen years since starting the business.

Sometimes it's better not to ask—or to listen—when people tell you something can't be done. I didn't ask for permission or approval. I just went ahead and did it.

MAKING IT OFFICIAL

On January 2, 1984, I went back to Austin earlier than I would have to attend classes, and I did all the things you need to do to set up a business. I registered the company with the State of Texas as "PC's Limited." I placed an ad in the classified section of our local newspaper.

Through previous contacts with customers and the small ad I

placed in the paper, I was already getting a lot of business. I was selling between $50,000 to $80,000 a month of upgraded PCs, upgrade kits, and add-on components to people in the Austin area. Not too long after starting school, I was able to move from a stuffy dorm room that I shared with a roommate to a condominium with high ceilings and two bedrooms. (I didn't, however, tell my parents for a few months that I had moved.)

In early May, about a week before I took final exams to complete my freshman year, I incorporated the company as "Dell Computer Corporation," doing business as "PC's Limited." The $1,000 required to capitalize a company in Texas was the extent of my initial start-up investment. We moved the business from my condo to a 1,000-square-foot office space in a small business center in North Austin. I hired a few people to take orders over the telephone and a few more people to fulfill them. Manufacturing consisted of three guys with screwdrivers sitting at six-foot tables upgrading machines. Business continued to grow, and I began to think hard about what the potential could be if I could devote myself to the venture, full-time.

Where I come from, not going to college is not an acceptable option. Convincing my parents to allow me to leave school would have been impossible. So I just went ahead and did it, whatever the consequences. I finished my freshman year, and left.

After a while, my parents forgave me. A little bit after that, I forgave them, too.

People ask me now, "Were you scared?" Sure. Nearly everyone's motivated by fear in some form. I was afraid that I wouldn't do a good job, that the business would be a complete failure. However, in my case, the downside was limited. The University of Texas had a great program that allowed students to take a semester off with no academic penalty. That gave me the freedom to start the business without worrying about closing the door completely on my education. With that in mind, I didn't have a lot to lose, other than missing a few fraternity parties. And if I couldn't make the business work, I could always return to my parents' original plan and go to medical school.

As it turned out, the timing for PC's Limited couldn't have been better. Around me, I saw people becoming more interested—and more knowledgeable—about computers and seeking more sophisticated versions of IBM PCs. But IBM wasn't producing them. In addition, anomalies in the distribution of these PCs had led to a tremendous imbalance in the demand and the supply. A dealer, for example, would order 100 computers and receive only 10. So the next time, to get what he wanted, he would order 1,000. Maybe then he'd get 633, when he'd needed only 100. He'd be stuck paying for the excess inventory, and as a result, would often sell the extras below their cost on what became known as the "IBM gray market." We would buy these stripped-down computers, add disk drives and memory, upgrade them, and sell them for a profit.

While this was a good business, in only seven or eight months it became clear that making our own PCs offered an even better opportunity. Reading through an electronics magazine one day, I saw a story about something called a chip set for a computer. Now everyone in the business knows what a chip set is, but when Gordon Campbell started a company called Chips & Technologies, the idea was new. He proposed to combine the 200 chips required to make a PC based on the Intel 286 microprocessor into only five or six ASIC (application specific integrated circuit) chips. Not only did the chip set very much simplify PC design, it enabled us to start making our own PCs starting with a couple of chip sets and a couple of engineers skilled in this area. (Of course, it turned out to be a much more complicated process, but the emergence of chip sets did ease our entry into the PC business.)

I contacted Campbell, got three or four chip sets, and put them on my desk as a reminder to do something about them. Then I contacted the local Intel salesperson and said, "Tell me who in this town can design a 286 computer."

I eventually got the names of six or seven engineers and groups of engineers who worked as teams. I called them up and explained that I wanted them to design a PC. I asked what it would cost, how long it would take, and what the risks were.

One engineer, Jay Bell, replied, "I can do it in about a week, week and a half, for $2,000."

"That doesn't sound like a lot to lose," I said. "I happen to be going out of town for a week. I'll give you $1,000 now and another $1,000 when I come back."

By the time I returned, Jay Bell had built our first 286-based PC. We were on our way.

GROWING PAINS

THERE WERE OBVIOUSLY NO CLASSES
on learning how to start and run a business in my high school,
so I clearly had a lot to learn. And learn I did, mostly by experimenting and making a bunch of mistakes. One of the first things I learned,
though, was that there was a relationship between screwing up and
learning: The more mistakes I made, the faster I learned. As you can
imagine, I was very *efficient*.

I tried to surround myself with smart advisors, and I tried not to
make the same mistake twice. Fortunately, I didn't make any huge
ones. However successful, the company was still so small that all of our
mistakes seemed kind of trivial—at least, in retrospect. Since we were
growing so quickly, everything was constantly changing. We'd say,
"What's the best way to do this?" and come up with an answer. The
resulting process would work for a while, then it would stop working

and we'd have to adjust it and try something else. For example, we had started by writing orders by hand and pinning them up on a clothesline. After a while, it became clear that this system couldn't handle the volume of orders coming in. So we hired a guy to write an order-entry program. But because our computers weren't networked, the salespeople would enter orders on their PCs and I would go around collecting the orders on diskettes and compile all of them into an order database. The whole thing was one big experiment.

I learned many valuable lessons along the way. Take delegation, for example. Since I had been a college student, I was used to a schedule that allowed me to sleep late. When I started the business, it was tough to get up early every morning. But I was the guy with the key, so if I overslept there would be twenty or thirty employees hanging around outside the door by the time I arrived, waiting for me to let them in. When I started the company, I rarely got the door open before nine-thirty. Then it was nine o'clock. Finally, we got started at eight A.M. And then I gave someone else the key.

Another time, I was in my office, busily trying to solve a complicated system problem, when an employee walked in, complaining that he had just lost a quarter in the Coke machine.

"Why are you telling me about it?" I asked.

"Because you've got the key to the Coke machine."

At that moment, I learned the value of giving someone else the key to the Coke machine.

THE GROWTH SPURT CONTINUES

Business was great, so, needless to say, we kept growing. Only one month after we'd moved into our 1,000-square-foot office, we moved to another that measured 2,350 square feet. After four or five months, we outgrew that and moved again, this time to a 7,200-square-foot space. Six months later, we moved again. We outgrew our telephone systems, our facilities, our organizational structures, every physical or electronic system we had. Finally, in 1985, we made the jump to a 30,000-square-foot building. It was as large as a football field, and I couldn't imagine that we'd ever fill it up. We weren't there even two years before we had to move again.

A lot of the elements that shaped—and continue to shape—our corporate culture were born during those early days. At the time, we were still a pretty high-risk venture, so we hired people who had a great sense of adventure and tended to be quite versatile. Of course, in certain areas, like finance, manufacturing, and information technology, we needed to hire people with specific expertise. But in other areas, we had more freedom. I remember sitting on the floor sorting through big stacks of resumes as if I were dealing cards, thinking, "Maybe this person would be good for this job, and this person for that one." Fortunately, there were a lot of talented people looking for jobs at the time. We recruited from local companies, from our competitors, and paid special attention to the University of Texas graduates who wanted to stay in the area. We knew even then that if you hired good people, they would bring more good people in their wake.

From the beginning, we tended to come at things in a very practical way. I was always asking, "What's the most efficient way to accomplish this?" Consequently, we eliminated the possibility for bureaucracy before it ever cropped up, and that provided opportunities for learning as well. Our sales force, for example, had to set up their own computers. They probably didn't enjoy it, but it gave them (and us) a real sense of what the uneducated customer would go through to set up his system, and it helped them develop a more intimate understanding of the products they were selling. As a result, they were able to help customers make informed decisions about what to buy *and* they could help solve equipment problems.

That marked the start of our reputation for great service, one of the tools for staying ahead of the competition.

By 1985, the industry had already become so intensely competitive that we had to keep innovating. Constantly questioning conventional thinking became part of our company mentality. And our explosive growth helped to foster a great sense of camaraderie and a real "can-do" attitude among our employees.

There were times when we were so tight on space that two people had to share one small cubicle. Engineers would help out when the manufacturing line got overloaded. Everyone pitched in and answered phones when the phone systems got backed up. Our salespeople would stuff RAM chips into tubes to ship to customers even while they were taking more orders on the phone. (At that time, random access memory chips came in little pieces that customers could add on to upgrade their PCs.)

We were also tight on money. People didn't have wastebaskets; instead, they used the cardboard boxes that computer parts came in. But they didn't seem to mind too much. We had the sense that we were doing something different, that we were part of something special. The spirit that today defines our company was beginning to take hold.

We challenged ourselves constantly, to grow more or to provide better service to our customers; and each time we set a new goal, we would make it. Then we'd stop for a moment, give each other a few high fives, and get started on tackling the next goal. People seemed to be energized by being around colleagues who had high expectations of themselves and of the company. The first day we did $1 million in sales, someone brought in cupcakes with "$1,000,000" written on each one. We tried to make it so that working at Dell wasn't just somewhere to spend time and collect a paycheck; it was fun, and often, an adventure.

In 1986, we hit a milestone when we hired Lee Walker as president. Lee, a venture capitalist who had also been an executive at a couple of other companies, was the first key management hire in the company's history. At the time, we were growing at a tremendous rate and were in great need of capital. One of the first things Lee did was to call up a buddy at Texas Commerce Bank and say, "I've got a neat company here, and you've got to give us a loan." Within eighteen hours, we had a decent line of credit.

Lee was also instrumental in shaping our Board of Directors when we became a public company in 1988. In trying to create a wish list of directors, we came up with two names: George Kozmetsky and Bob Inman. Both lived in Austin, had a knowledge of the computer industry, and had very distinguished backgrounds. George was a cofounder of Teledyne and had served as dean of the University of Texas School of Business; Bob had been chairman, president, and CEO of Westmark Systems, a private defense company, and had extensive background in the federal government. Lee and I each took a name and went after them, and after hearing what we'd accomplished so far, they agreed to join. Their presence gave us a huge boost in credibility; young companies like Dell typically don't have such a strong board starting out. As the original Board members, George and Bob set a precedent of sage advice and valuable counsel that has helped carry us to where we are today.

THE DIRECT MODEL, VERSION 1.0

Because we were constantly talking with both prospective customers and people who had already bought our products, we knew exactly what they wanted, what they were happy with, and where we could make improvements. It had always made more sense to me to build a business based on what people *really* wanted, rather than guess at what we thought they might want. For us it was partly a necessity, because we started out with so little capital and didn't have the extra time or the resources to fool around with excess inventory.

That marked the official beginning of what we call the "direct model."

From the start, our entire business—from design to manufacturing to sales—was oriented around listening to the customer, responding to the customer, and delivering what the customer wanted. Our direct relationship—first through telephone calls, then through face-to-face interactions, and now through the Internet—has enabled us to benefit from real-time input from real customers regarding product and service requirements, products on the market, and future products they would like to see developed.

The direct model is based on direct selling—not using a reseller or the retail channel—and it's not new. But the way we went about it was quite different. Mainframes and minicomputers were originally sold directly, but because dealing direct required somewhat of an expensive and cumbersome organizational structure, most computer manufacturers sold directly only to their best and largest accounts. They used the retail channel or resellers to sell to their lower-volume customers. We, however, sold—and continue to sell—directly to all our customers, including more than 400 of the Fortune 500.

While other companies had to guess which products their customers wanted, because they built them in advance of taking the order, we *knew*—because our customers told us *before* we built the product.

While other companies had to estimate which configurations were the most popular, we knew, based upon whether our customers ordered one floppy drive or two, or one floppy drive and a hard drive. We could build the product to meet their exact needs.

Other companies had to maintain high levels of inventory to stock the reseller and retail channels. Because we built only what our customers wanted when they wanted it, we didn't have a lot of inventory taking up space and soaking up capital. Because we didn't have the extra cost of the dealer or the associated inventory, we were able to offer great value to our customers and expand rapidly. And with every new customer, we gathered more information about their product and service requirements. It was the perfect closed loop.

There's a real productivity advantage in the direct model because of the way the sales cycle works. In the indirect model, there are two sales forces: sales from the manufacturer to the dealer, and sales from the dealer to the customer. In the direct model, we have just one sales force, and it's totally focused on the customer.

And not just any customer—but a specific type of customer. We quickly realized that there was a big difference between selling to large corporations and selling to individual consumers. So we hired salespeople who had the experience to sell face to face to large corporations. Other salespeople became experts at selling to federal and state governments, or educational institutions, or small companies and individual consumers.

We discovered, too, that there was a massive sales advantage to this structure because our salespeople were specialists. They didn't have to try to learn everything there was to know about eight different products from eight different manufacturers. They also didn't need to remember the product preferences of every different type of account. And while that was an obvious relief to our sales force, it was also beneficial to our customers. Their specific salespeople could cater directly to their needs, questions, and preferences, enhancing their overall experience with Dell.

As a natural extension of customer contact, the direct model allows us to take the pulse of whatever market we move into and provide the right technology for the right customers. The direct model has become the backbone of our company and the greatest tool in its growth.

It all evolved from the basic idea of eliminating the middleman.

FASTER, BIGGER, BETTER

We weren't, obviously, the only company to build IBM-compatible PCs. A whole industry of suppliers was emerging to help companies enter the computer business. While we were the first company selling direct, we weren't the only one; and still, many customers weren't really sure what to make of us. We needed to further differentiate ourselves from the army of companies jumping into the PC business.

One of the biggest barriers to selling direct was that many potential customers had a perfectly understandable fear of shelling out $4,000 to a company they'd never heard of without a physical store they could walk into. So we advertised a thirty-day money-back guarantee for our products. Promoting our guarantee helped dispel our customers' fears and gave Dell a reputation for reliability.

Quality was another big differentiator. Sometimes we'd find incompatibilities in the components from our suppliers and would have to go back to them to ensure they met our standards. But the problems often continued. So we dedicated more resources toward designing PCs that were compatible with IBM's and had the highest-quality components. We formed close relationships with our suppliers, teaching them our requirements, sharing testing and validation data, and driving them for continuous improvement.

Designing our own products also meant that we could enhance their performance. At the time, performance was the name of the game, and if you could make an IBM-compatible PC that was faster than the IBM PC, it obviously would give you a distinct edge over the competition. We knew there was a lot of enthusiasm for designs that would push the speed limit. So we deduced: If IBM had 70 percent of the PC market using a 6 megahertz 286 PC, we had to come out with an 8 megahertz machine.

We ended up building a 12 megahertz machine.

We had actually achieved 16 megahertz in the lab, but felt that 12 megahertz was something we could produce in volume. We could now offer the best service, quality, *and* performance. So we ran a two-page ad in *PC Week* and *PC Magazine* comparing our 12 megahertz

ell.com **www.dell.com** www.dell.com www.dell.com www.dell.com www.dell.

machine (priced at $1,995) to IBM's 6 megahertz machine (priced at $3,995). Then we went to spring Comdex '86.

Comdex back then was a show mostly for computer dealers and resellers, and it was unusual for a company that sold direct to attend. Fortunately, we managed to secure the last remaining booth in the main arena when another company cancelled. We threw together a display that showed a brick wall made of Styrofoam with our 12 MHz 286 breaking through to signify that we had broken through the 12 megahertz barrier. It looked kind of rinky-dink compared to the glitzy displays from Compaq and IBM, but that didn't matter. We had the fastest-performing machine by far.

Soon after the show opened, two long lines of people stacked up at our booth. In one line was the press, collectively scratching its head and wondering why anyone would *want* a computer that fast. In the other were all of the people who were totally thrilled by the concept of a high-performance machine and wanted to know how to get one.

The Comdex show taught us the value of performance and time to market. From out of nowhere, we were thrust into the spotlight because we had a leading machine ready to go well ahead of the competition. We went from being buried on page 87 of *PC Week* to being featured on the cover.

Of course, performance and time to market are huge differentiators, and highlighted the efficiency of what we were doing. By this time, we had also developed a reputation for great service and support, as well as great value. It caused our customers to ask the question, "Now, remind me again why we should pay all this money to a dealer for a slower machine?" No one could ignore the tremendous value we were bringing to the market.

The momentum continued as the press took notice and began reviewing our systems. Our computers started winning performance awards. We began receiving five stars for quality, support, and service. All the key magazines began recommending Dell for best value and highest performance. We began to attract increasing numbers of knowledgeable business customers, who were always the core of our market.

We had arrived in corporate America.

THE CRISIS OF SUCCESS

By the end of 1986, Dell was doing about $60 million in sales. Business was booming and we had increased our recognition exponentially. But we were concerned about what would happen next.

Our success was, in fact, something of a crisis point. Investment bankers started calling and saying, "Why don't you go public?" Venture capitalists were calling and saying, "Want some capital?" Other companies showed up to see if we wanted to sell. It was clear that great opportunities lay ahead. But we were concerned that we could not achieve them if we just kept doing what we were doing. We had to do something dramatically different.

I decided to call a brainstorming meeting in the fall of '86, to be held in the California wine country, for key company executives and thought leaders from both inside and outside the industry to try to figure out how best to evolve the business. There was certainly an element of risk in exposing our strategies and weaknesses to industry luminaries like Jim Seymour and Esther Dyson, but I knew their fresh perspective and advice would more than compensate for that.

We asked questions like: Where is the company today? What do we think it will become? Where do we want it to go? What are the opportunities that can take us there and how can we take advantage of them? We came up with a 131-item wish list.*

---

*Looking back, I'm delighted to see that we've achieved almost all of the items on the list over time—except for the one where customers could talk to a personal robot whose voice would be provided by Catherine Deneuve.

In addition to the wish list, three key realizations came out of that meeting. The first: To really grow our business, we would have to target large companies. The second: To land large companies, we would have to offer the absolute best support in the industry. That was how we came up with the idea to provide the industry's first on-site service for personal computers—and rather than fool around too much with the logistics, one day we just started providing it. If a customer called us with a problem, we'd say, "We'll be out tomorrow to fix it." This was in contrast to the alternative, which required the customer to either bring the PC to a dealer, or worse yet, send it back to the factory.

It's always been our nature to think about what is possible and what is achievable, and set stretch goals accordingly. The goal we set in that meeting was to achieve $1 billion in sales by 1992. That was a pretty awesome goal. But we did the math: We figured that between the present market and the potential market, given the quality of our products and our own market share, the goal was realistic.

All we had to do was figure out how to achieve it.

INNOCENTS ABROAD

The third big idea to come out of that brainstorming meeting was for global expansion. We knew we had to expand our business outside the U.S., but the company was only two and half years old and we had very little capital. I remember going back to the office after the brainstorming meeting and telling people that we were going to expand internationally. They thought we were absolutely crazy.

We didn't just decide to blanket the globe, however. We looked carefully at the markets in Canada, the United Kingdom, Germany, and France. We briefly considered Japan, but realized it was more of a longer-term dream. The investment we'd need to enter a market that was then dominated by entrenched Japanese companies was more than we could handle. And while Canada represented an easier, safer option, it wasn't going to help us get established in Europe, which I knew held incredible potential.

Two years earlier, I'd been to London for a family vacation during the spring break of my freshman year in college. My older brother was living there for six months between graduating from college and going to medical school. I had taken the opportunity to roam into a couple of computer stores, and I observed the same high markup/lousy service phenomenon in the United Kingdom as I had in the United States. We decided to expand into the U.K. first for this reason, as well as the language factor. Our move couldn't have been more timely.

Just as in the U.S., there were a number of companies in the U.K. selling cheap computers that didn't work very well. Nevertheless, they sold a lot of them. What was important about this was that we knew there were many people in the U.K. who wanted PCs but were faced with products and service that were unsatisfactory. These companies effectively created a knowledgeable market that was primed to buy from Dell.

Dell U.K. opened for business in June 1987. Of the twenty-two journalists who came to our press announcement, about twenty-one predicted that we would fail. The direct model is an American concept, they claimed; nobody will buy computers direct from the manufacturer.

It's a bad idea, they said. Go home.

But the customers set their own rules. They knew what they wanted, and they knew we could provide it. The business was profitable from its very first days, and now Dell U.K. is almost a $2-billion-a-year company.

In thinking about our early philosophies of "thinking unconventionally" and "not listening to people who tell you something can't be done," it's interesting to note that many people told us the direct model would fail in virtually every country we expanded into over the next ten years. The message was always the same: Our country is different, your business model won't work here. The nay-saying eventually started to die down as we completed our expansion into western and central Europe, but it started right up again when we moved into Asia. There it took a slightly different turn. This is a Western concept, they told us. It won't work here, go home. But rather than tailoring the strategy to fit the culture, we said, "We think the direct model will work cross-culturally. And we're willing to take the risk."

To be sure, we do some localization. You obviously can't sell English-language computers in China. And from a cultural perspective, customers in other countries are different. We learned, for example, that some Germans aren't comfortable telephoning in a response to an advertisement; they find it too forward. They will, however, respond to an ad that features a fax number. They'll send in a fax, asking for more information, and will provide their name and phone number so that a Dell representative can call them. The conversation that ensues is almost exactly the same as that which would have occurred if the German customer had made the call himself. It was a slight modification that allowed us to adapt to cultural differences without altering our business strategies.

There were also some countries where our local management didn't completely understand the core strategy and tried to build a hybrid that wasn't quite our direct business model. Not only did they not succeed, but they stalled the eventual success of Dell in those markets. We've since corrected that. The lesson is: Believe in what you're doing. If you've got an idea that's really powerful, you've just got to ignore the people who tell you it won't work, and hire people who embrace your vision.

WHAT A TIME TO GO PUBLIC

At about that time, we also started to think about raising capital through a public stock offering. We needed some capital to grow the company, to get better credit with our suppliers, and to establish credibility with our large customers by becoming more of a peer. In order to finance our aggressive expansion into the corporate market, we needed capital to fund receivables that would be larger and, we hoped, more numerous than any we had had before.

Then-president Lee Walker and I invited interested investment bankers to meetings at our Austin headquarters. Each would have a better story than the next about what they could do for us and the rewards we would reap. Lee and I would look at each other and say, "These guys are full of it. They're just telling us what they think we want to hear." After looking long and hard at each of the firms, we settled on Goldman Sachs. Why? We especially liked their recommendation of *not* going public. Instead, they suggested that we first consider a private offering with a small group of investors. We could then wait until the company grew a little more and we had more experience in dealing with the challenges presented to a public company. *Then* we could go public, if we wanted. It wasn't the answer we thought we were going to get, but it turned out to be exactly the right one.

The private placement memorandum was published in July 1987. It summarized what we had achieved in three years. It read:

> Dell Computer Corporation designs, develops, markets, manufactures, supports and services technically advanced, IBM-compatible personal computers. Its products are currently sold under the "PC's Limited" brand name directly to end-users. The Company's customers are primarily medium and small-sized businesses and individuals and, to a lesser extent, multinational corporations, government agencies and academic institutions. Since its inception in 1984, Dell has sold over $160 million of computers and related equipment on an initial invested capital base of only $1,000. The

Company has been profitable in every quarter of its existence, and sales have increased in each quarter since the
Company's inception.

The memorandum went on to list and describe the three key
strengths that gave us a competitive advantage:

◆ Our ability to produce a line of high-performance products
   compatible with accepted IBM standards. (In fact, many of our
   products had performance features that were superior to IBM
   systems, and were frequently top-ranked by publications such
   as *PC Magazine* and *PC World*.)

◆ Our direct relationship marketing concept: "With an average of
   approximately 1,400 telephone calls received daily, Dell gets
   real-time input from its customers regarding their product and
   service requirements, their views on various products in the
   market, and their response to Company advertising. This input
   gives the Company a competitive advantage in tailoring its
   product offerings and communications programs to meet its
   customers' needs. Direct relationship marketing also eliminates
   the 25% to 45% dealer mark-up, thereby enabling the
   Company to price its products aggressively. In addition, the
   Company's marketing strategy allows it to sell its products
   through Company employees who are trained specifically to
   sell Dell products."

◆ Our ability to maintain an efficient and flexible manufacturing
   operation resulting in a streamlined asset base. We didn't have
   much in the way of capital, and our inventory was unusually
   low because we built our machines to customers' orders and
   not to dealers' forecasts.

By October 1987, we were ready to raise $20 million. Just as we were ready to close the deal, the stock market crashed. I thought we were doomed. What's amazing, though, is that because of the strength of our business strategy and our results, the crash had little meaningful impact on investors' participation in the private placement. On the morning of Black Monday, our subscription was $23 million; when we closed the deal a couple of days later, it was $21 million and change.

Out of the thousands of deals that were supposed to be done, ours actually happened because investors had real faith in our company.

The private financing set us up well, and the following June we went public. We raised $30 million; the market value of the company was about $85 million.

We had done this in three years, starting with an idea, $1,000, and a college dorm room.

LESSONS LEARNED—AND NOT

Twelve years after it was written, it's interesting to read over the private placement memorandum. We're now a $30 billion company, but the key strengths that gave us a competitive advantage then are still absolutely central to our existence.

We learned to identify our core strengths. Pretty early on in the company's life, we concluded that we wanted to earn a reputation for providing great customer service, as well as great products. The idea was that building a business solely on cost or price was not a sustainable advantage. There would always be someone with something that was lower in price or cheaper to produce. What was really important was sustaining loyalty among customers and employees, and that could only be derived from having the highest level of service and very high-performing products.

We put a great deal of emphasis on understanding what drove customer satisfaction, whether it was response times on the telephone, quality of products, valuable features, or the ease of experience in using the product. Engaging the entire company—from manufacturing to engineering to sales to support staff—in the process of understanding customer requirements became a constant focus of management energy, training, and employee education.

We learned the importance of ignoring conventional wisdom and doing things our way. When we were completing our private stock placement in 1987, a noted industry analyst said we would never grow beyond $150 million in revenue. He was only off by a few zeros.

It's fun to do things that people don't think are possible or likely. It's also exciting to achieve the unexpected. Our competitors didn't consider us a threat for a long time, providing us with an even greater opportunity to surprise them with our success.

Finally, we learned to be opportunistic. What I saw as an opportunity to create a more efficient business system turned into a model that has in some ways revolutionized the way our industry conducts business.

At our brainstorming meeting in 1986, we had projected revenues of $1 billion by 1992. At the time, that seemed like a major stretch goal. In fact, by 1992 we were doing twice that amount.

The direct model has enabled us to achieve incredible success. But in today's competitive world, a brilliant business model alone doesn't create a sustainable advantage. And over the next couple of years, we would discover that what we didn't learn during our start-up phase was nearly as important as what we did.

We would soon be faced with challenges that would threaten the very existence of our company.

LEARNING THE HARD WAY

IT'S BEEN SAID THAT A STRENGTH, WHEN used to excess, can become a weakness. Was that ever true for us. By the end of the 1980s and into the early 90s, Dell was coming off a major growth high. Our sales had grown at a compounded annual rate of 97 percent and net income had grown even faster, at a compounded annual rate of 166 percent. At the time, it seemed as though growth was our greatest strength. And to some extent, it was. But what we didn't realize was that, in the young life of Dell Computer, growth was the only thing we'd ever known. As success followed on success, it was hard to imagine that growth would at some point become our greatest vulnerability.

We had built the company around a systematic process: give customers the high-quality computers they want at a competitive price as quickly as possible, backed by great service. Because of that—and because we were still relatively small—the opportunities for growth seemed limitless, and we became accustomed to pursuing them.

We didn't understand that with every new growth opportunity came a commensurate level of risk—a lesson we learned the hard way.

DISDAINING INVENTORY

Dell was founded on the premise of "under-promise and over-deliver"—to customers, employees, and suppliers. We had also built our reputation, in part, on how well we managed our inventory, which led to faster service and greater savings for our customers. So it probably seems somewhat peculiar that the first meaningful setback we experienced in 1989 had to do with having too *much* inventory.

Because we were used to chasing after every incremental dollar of growth, our sales were rising very, very quickly. Naturally, we saw this as a positive sign. And to fill this demand, we of course had to buy parts—among them, memory chips. But instead of buying the right number of memory chips—which we would today—we bought as many of those suckers as we could get our hands on.

Those of you familiar with the concept of "demand chain management" know what happened next.

We bought more chips than we needed, at the peak of a cyclical market. And then prices plunged. To make matters worse, we also got caught "crossing the street" technologically, as memory chip capacity went from 256K to 1 megabyte almost overnight.

We were suddenly stuck with too many chips that nobody wanted—not to mention the fact that they had cost us a ton of money. There we were, the company that had been built on dealing direct, trapped in the very same inventory quandary that had been plaguing our indirect competitors.

Inventory is the worst thing to own in an industry in which the value of materials or information declines quickly, which today means any industry—from computers, to airlines, to fashion. In the electronics industry, for example, the rapid pace of technological change can sink the value of inventory you're holding over the course of days. In the information industry, the value of information can decline in hours or minutes, or even seconds, as it does if you're in the financial markets. As one of my colleagues in this industry likes to say, inventory has the shelf life of lettuce.

And when you're not yet an industry leader, managing inventory becomes even harder. Back in '89, we didn't have the vendor relationships we have today, which could have helped us negotiate a situation like that more gracefully. We didn't have the forecasting skills we have today, and we didn't have the disdain for inventory that we do now—which was born, in part, of that experience.

We had to sell off that inventory, which depressed our earnings to the point where the company earned only a penny per share in one quarter. To compensate, we had to raise the price of our products, slowing our growth. And we had to postpone plans to launch operations in new countries. For the first time in the company's history, we didn't deliver. To our stunned disbelief, we had quickly become known as the company with the inventory problem.*

The inventory problem was definitely a huge heads-up to us, forcing us to pace ourselves better and rediscover one of the building blocks of our success: the value and importance of managing inventory. Out of this experience, we learned that improving the speed of our inventory flow is not only a winning strategy but a necessity: It combats the rapid decline in the value of materials and requires less cash and has less risk. We also made a greater commitment to understanding and utilizing forecasting.

Today people sometimes ask me if, during this time, I was scared.

---

*Since then, we have moved from last place in inventory management to first place.

Of course I was. Having disappointed our customers, employees, and shareholders, I was worried about losing their trust. But I was also scared because, for the first time, I started thinking I might be in over my head.

A LESSON OF OLYMPIC PROPORTIONS

The next crisis—or "lesson," as we like to think of it—didn't reassure me much. If the inventory problem was diametrically opposed to our strength as a direct seller, the Olympic lesson was just as perplexing, as we had always been a company that took pride in—and direction from—customer feedback.

Based upon what we now recognize (somewhat facetiously) as a "misjudgment of the importance of certain technological features," we devised a plan to launch a family of products code-named "Olympic." Aptly named for its enormous scope, Olympic was what we technology people call a "boil the ocean" product: It spanned the desktop, workstation, and server markets and proposed to do—well, pretty much everything. It was an incredibly ambitious plan, and the first really large development project we'd undertaken. And it made sense at the time, as we thought we could capitalize on some of our key strengths in those markets. The possibilities were seductive; if we could pull Olympic off, it would put us on the map for having created the broadest product line ever and would lead us to a huge wave of growth.

What we didn't realize was that bleeding-edge technology was the last thing we needed.

With great enthusiasm, we started introducing what we thought were Olympic's terrific features to our customers. They weren't terribly impressed.

"Some things about it are compelling," they said. "But the whole product in and of itself isn't compelling *enough*. I'll pass." We could barely believe what we were hearing—truth is, we didn't want to believe it—so at first we denied it. We proceeded to prepare prototypes to show at the annual Comdex trade show in November 1989, and with some fanfare, we unveiled them there.

Our customers said, "So what? We don't need that much technology. Thanks anyway."

We knew that technologically, this product line made sense. There were ideas within it that made for great inventions, like the graphics and disk technology that were later incorporated into highly successful products; that, however, just wasn't enough. We weren't then—and we certainly aren't now—in the business of convincing people to buy something they didn't want, so we canceled Olympic before it ever saw the light of day, and admitted we made a mistake. We had gone ahead and created a product that was, for all intents and purposes, technology for technology's sake, rather than technology for the customer's sake. If we had consulted our customers first about what *they* needed—as we had been accustomed to doing—we could have saved ourselves a lot of time and aggravation.

Two valuable lessons emerged out of this misstep: No matter what your industry, try to identify potential problems early—and fix them fast. And involve your customers early in the developmental process. They are your most valuable focus group. Listen early and listen well.

CREATING TECHNOLOGY FOR THE CUSTOMER'S SAKE

We also learned that this theory of "big bang product development" was not something we wanted to be involved in. Instead, gradual and incremental improvements to each individual product line were a far better choice for us for two main reasons: It reduced our risk and allowed us to take advantage of rapid technological transitions, offering the fastest, best components available. In the big picture, we began realizing that we needed to pace our investments to match our progress—that financially, we weren't the little upstart start-up we once had been, and we needed to think carefully about what opportunities would be best for us in the long run.

The Olympic experience definitely helped to refocus the way we thought about research and development. The traditional approach in our industry is, "If we build it, they will come." But rather than build something and hope for the best, we now set our sights on designing products based only on clear customer need and input.

Things changed as a result of the Olympic experience. For one thing, we started thinking and talking in terms of "relevant technology," a phrase we used to describe the features that were important to our customers. For another, we consciously committed to a set of principles regarding "buy versus make"; there were times when it made the most sense to leave the R&D to our suppliers, and times when it made sense to invent things ourselves. This philosophy helped guide our decisions, and caused us to focus on how best to use our engineers.

The scope of the Olympic project had led us to recruit and develop a large cadre of very talented engineers. When we canceled Olympic, we could have easily said, "These people developed this thing that nobody wants to buy. Let's just get rid of them and start over." Instead, we concluded that our engineers were, in fact, brilliant; they just hadn't known what our customers wanted. Given the right input, goals, and direction, we trusted that they would be able to create terrific products that our customers would love.

But this line of thought—and the concept behind "buy versus make"—led to an interesting quandary for some of our engineers. We encouraged them to get to know customers' needs by spending time with representatives from sales, we involved them more in product planning so that they could be exposed to the logic of the decision-making process, and we tried to train them to think in terms of what their contribution meant to the overall business. Some resisted, saying "I don't want to do that, I just want to design silicon." But some really thrived. Teaching bright technical people to think beyond the technology and in terms of what people really want—and what makes for good business—isn't always easy. It can take time, but it can best be done by immersing them in the buying process and involving them in the strategy and logic that go into deciding what creates value for customers. And it's incredibly gratifying to watch a brilliant technologist grow to understand all aspects of the way our business works.

Paradoxically, the worst thing—and the best thing—about the Olympic project was that it was such an ambitious effort. Taken all together, it was simply too big in scope and concept; but in truth, some genuinely valuable inventions were born during its course.

The demands of Olympic caused us to build up resources in our technology and product development organizations. By focusing our R&D organization on relevant technology, and deciding what not to make ourselves, we were able to deliver a fantastic array of products over the next several years that led to a huge wave of growth. In fact, we had our largest single product launch ever a few months after we disbanded the Olympic project. The launch included our first high-end floor-standing systems and advanced storage options—both of which incorporated technologies developed during the Olympic program. Thanks to our customers, we turned a potentially disastrous mistake into a great opportunity, and pushed the company to the forefront of technological development.

TO GROW, OR NOT TO GROW

After the inventory and Olympic fiascos were behind us—from 1990 through 1992—Dell Computer enjoyed three glorious years of growth. The direct model strategy was working well. Our growth rate had risen from 50 percent to more than 100 percent per year, and we were earning a 5 percent profit on sales.* The company was introducing new desktops and notebooks, and even took its first foray into servers. We had expanded all over western and central Europe and were planning to launch operations in Asia.

Our potential seemed limitless.

Boy, were we ill-prepared for what we had coming.

In retrospect, it's easy to talk about managing rapid growth. But on a day-to-day basis, you hardly notice how fast—or how slowly—you're growing. You walk into the office, you talk to customers, you work to develop products, you expand into other countries. It's not like there are sirens going off or people running through the hallways saying, "You're growing too fast! Stop!" In fact, while it's happening, it seems to happen in slow motion.

There were, however, industry forces at work that were causing me some concern as far as our growth rate went. And that had to do with the probability of consolidation.

In the U.S., corporate customers were looking to narrow their choices—they didn't want to buy from eight different PC vendors. Consumers were becoming more discriminating about brands and service. All over the world, there were PC companies that were strong enough to survive on their own. Some companies had a strong distribution; others offered a solid brand; but many, like Tulip in the Netherlands and Olivetti in Italy and Siemens in Germany, were one-country hero companies, creating products exclusively tailored for their markets without being globally competitive.

We believed they would disappear in the consolidation of the PC

---

*Five percent was actually lower than what some of our competitors were earning on sales, but our competitors weren't growing at the same rate. We felt we needed a growth strategy more than a profit maximization strategy at that point in our development.

industry. And because of our size, we were afraid the same thing might happen to us.

At this critical juncture, I realized we had to decide whether we should stay the size we were—and face the consequences—or go for big-time growth. Though we were at $1 billion in sales at the time, it didn't really matter. We were not growing in increments that would allow us to be large enough to compete on a global level when the market really started to consolidate, and it was clearly going to—soon.

If we stayed the size we were, we wouldn't be able to amortize our development costs over a large enough volume, and our cost structure would be too high. We'd run the risk of being uncompetitive, and we could easily get left in the dust.

We needed a new game plan—and fast.

STAY TRUE TO YOUR TALENTS

Obviously, we went for growth—in one big leap.

One of our strategies for growth was to move into the retail channel. This decision was not based on following the truth of our convictions—or even what we knew to be our core competencies—but basically, because we panicked. At this point in time, all of our competitors were selling indirectly through dealers and resellers. They, too, were concerned about consolidation, but they were larger than we were, and certainly more established. The industry buzz was that Dell could not continue to grow by direct sales of computers alone; rather, that only by combining our direct business with sales of software, accessories, and computers in retail outlets, would we stand a chance.

After violating two of the three golden Dell rules—1) Disdain inventory, and 2) Always listen to the customer—we were about to denigrate the third:

Never sell indirect.

Rather than stay true to what we knew, we listened to what people told us—at least enough to experiment in this new venue. We started selling computers through CompUSA (then known as Soft Warehouse) and some of the superstores, such as the Price Club and Sam's. Our PCs were selling well through the clubs and retail channels, even though at the time we had no real sense as to whether or not we were actually making any money on them.

It would take a few years—and a lot of homework—to truly appreciate just what an advantage we had with the direct model.

While we knew that the direct model was a differentiator for us in the industry, there was, in 1991, another. Late in the year, we began to convert our entire desktop product line to feature Intel's 486 microprocessor.

At this time, new levels of processing power had begun to drive waves of industry growth. It was around the same time that Microsoft's Windows operating system was really catching on, gaining incredible market penetration. Customers needed and wanted more powerful computers that could run Windows efficiently.

Since we had converted our product line to the 486, we realized we had a real advantage. We also recognized that the window of opportunity during which we could accelerate our growth rate and get the company firing on all cylinders was small. We had heard that our competitors were about to introduce lower-cost PCs, and that some were going to start selling their products directly. We had to move fast.

In 1992, we adopted an aggressive pricing strategy in an effort to drive growth rates. And succeed we did. In that year alone, we grew from $890 million to slightly more than $2 billion, an astronomical rate of 127 percent. We knew there was such a thing as growing too fast, but we also knew that if we didn't do it, we might not live to tell about it.

By the end of 1992, our growth initiative had gotten too strong. We were pulling in more than $2 billion in revenue but we still had the infrastructure of a $500 million company. Just about every system we had installed a couple of years before was now unable to support our business. We had outgrown our phone system, our basic financial system, our support system, and our parts numbering system. Our factory systems were all stretched well beyond their original capacity.

Most important, we had outgrown some of our people. We didn't have people with the experience of running a $2 billion-plus company. We simply couldn't keep up with our accelerating growth.

By now, I *knew* I needed help.

FINDING OUR FOOTING

IF WE HAD STAYED A SMALL PC COMPANY, we would have been killed.

However, rapid growth causes its own conundrum. If you build an infrastructure for a $3 billion company before you get there, it'll inevitably weigh you down to the point that you *don't* get there. You've got to have the confidence in yourself and in the opportunity, and you've got to build the infrastructure as you grow. That's how we did it. And I don't know that there was a better alternative.

Like many companies, we were always focused on our profit and loss statement. But cash flow was not a regularly discussed topic. It was as if we were driving along, watching only the speedometer, when in fact we were running out of gas.

We had gone from a fairly simple business in one or two markets to a much broader business that featured many more product lines, channels, and geographies. We didn't understand the economics of all those businesses, either at that moment in time or over a longer period, nor did we have the systems or management in place to oversee them all. We were consuming huge amounts of cash, while our profitability began to deteriorate, and both our inventory and our accounts receivable were piling up.

By early 1993, I had begun to feel as if all the news I heard was bad news. After many years of success, and then trying hard to weather the frequent storms of the previous few years, I couldn't help but think, "What happened? And why?"

Fortunately, we didn't waste any time denying that we had a problem or trying to explain it away. The root cause was obvious. As we had learned to do with the Olympic project and other problems after it, both big and small, we cut right to the chase and set about fixing the problem—fast.

Part of the fix was Tom Meredith. We had hired Tom from Sun Microsystems to become our new chief financial officer in November 1992. During the interviews, Tom had warned me that it was just a matter of time before Dell hit the wall. And while I knew that there were problems, I told him at the time he was an alarmist. By 1993, however, it looked as though he had been right.

We had planned to issue a secondary public offering of stock in early 1993 to give us some liquidity. But our stock price was down to $30.08, so we canceled the offering. That didn't help our cash flow. We subsequently posted our first and only quarterly loss in the company's history.

We had been operating under the assumption that we would grow faster than the market, but that we would still achieve a return on sales of 5 percent. But we had grown *too* quickly. We realized our priorities had to change. We needed to focus on slow, steady growth, and liquidity. Once we got our cash situation in order, we could then turn on the profit valve and eventually reaccelerate our growth. Instead of "growth,

growth, growth," the new order of business at Dell would be "liquidity, profitability, and growth"—in that order.

Achieving this was a laborious but revealing process. We analyzed each and every segment of our business carefully, with the hope of coming up with a profit and loss statement for each *part* of it. By understanding the economics of each segment of our business, we could appropriately target our best opportunities and where we needed to improve.

Our new focus on liquidity, profitability, and growth became a company-wide goal. Each manager embarked upon the "cash and profit hunt," in an effort to come up with a plan to reduce costs, build sales, and increase cash flow. At management meetings, I would hand out pyramid-shaped Plexiglas paperweights with the Dell logo in the middle and "liquidity," "profitability," and "growth" on each point.

The cash and profit hunt also was important because it forced our managers to take responsibility for the total performance of their business. Suddenly, we were asking them to think not just about how to grow the business, but also about how it could be more profitable and efficient with its assets. In some cases, the concept was as foreign to many managers as learning the business side of different things was to some engineers.

As a start-up, we'd been willing to try lots of things. And obviously, where product and technological innovation were concerned, we would still put a high priority on being experimental and innovative. But as far as focusing the business was concerned, our mandate was clear: We needed to get serious.

Once we established clear metrics and measurements, it was easy to see which businesses were performing or not, and to change the strategy accordingly. For example, we changed our information systems so that a salesperson could see the level of margin for a product literally as he or she was selling it on the phone. Or consider sales compensation. Previously, you might have had a case where two salespeople would each sell $1 million worth of our products, but one might have a 28 percent profit margin and the other only 8 percent. Our improved sales compensation system emphasized profit margins, and since the margins determined the sales representatives' compensation, they were heavily motivated to change.

We instituted the practice of strong profit and loss management. By demanding a detailed P&L for each business unit, we learned the incredible value of facts and data in managing a complex business. As we have grown, Dell has become a highly data- and P&L-driven company, values that have since become core to almost everything we do.

INTO THE EYE OF THE STORM

At the same time we were dealing with the cash flow crisis, we also began experiencing problems with our notebook computers. This was another reason why in early 1993, I felt as if every piece of news I got was bad.

We had gone into the notebook market in 1988 and had quickly developed an impressive reputation. We were first to market with a notebook based on Intel's 486 microprocessor, which featured one of the first color displays. We also had introduced one of the thinnest and lightest subnotebook computers available. But as our products got increasingly more ambitious in their technical complexity, it became apparent to me that we didn't have the capability inside the company to get the products to market on time, much less designed correctly.

The first difficulty we encountered was with the design of a new product. Basically, our approach to designing notebooks was almost exactly the same as our approach to designing desktops, which makes about as much sense as treating children like mini-adults. Strange as it sounds, this happened in large part simply because some engineers from our desktop division transferred into notebooks.

Clearly, this wasn't the right way to approach the design. Designing a desktop is not the same as designing a portable computer. In a desktop there are between thirty and thirty-five parts; in an average notebook, there are twice as many. And the parts don't all work together in a portable the way they do in a desktop PC.

In April 1993, we hired John Medica, who had led the development of Apple's PowerBook, to take charge of our notebook division. By the time he arrived, we had already canceled one product, but we still had several products in development, the design of which seemed to be taking longer than expected.* One of the first things John did when he arrived at Dell was to make a realistic assessment of the products in development. He wanted to get a sense of what was near completion, and why things were taking so long.

What he found was that only one of our products in development—the Latitude XP—would actually be competitive.

We were clearly in a dilemma. Selling notebooks would have obviously helped generate cash and increase profitability; canceling products in development would be painful and costly. But we could not sell something that wasn't ready and that our customers wouldn't like. We also knew, though, that correcting the products by redesigning them, validating the new design, manufacturing them, and delivering them would have taken so long that by the time we got them out the door, we'd be at the tail end of the product life cycle.

It really was a no-win situation. So, based on John's recommendation, we made a hard decision. We canceled several products that were in development and focused almost all of our energy on the one remaining design.

There was never any question, however, of whether to get out of notebooks altogether. The notebook market at the time was the

---

*The delay was due to feature creep, which occurs when too many features are added to a product until, ultimately, it becomes overdesigned.

fastest-growing segment of the industry and one of the most prof-itable. And we had lots of customers who depended on us to fulfill our commitments. But for a while we were caught between past and future products with nothing new to sell. When customers asked to see our notebook computers, we actually had to say, "We don't have anything to show right now but we have something coming soon." Then we described our plan to fix the notebook situation.

And while other areas within the company were doing well, morale in the notebook group was, as you'd expect, pretty poor. The engineers had spent a lot of time developing the products we'd just canceled, and they felt frustrated and demoralized when their hard work wasn't brought to fruition.

As the company leader, I did the only thing I could. I reinforced our strategy to the notebook group, and encouraged them to pull together to ensure that the Latitude XP stayed on track. To prove our commitment to the market, we found a partner with whom we worked to quickly develop and introduce a more basic notebook product that held us over until we were back up to speed.

Focusing on Latitude was ultimately a healthy experience for all of us, as it distracted us from the otherwise painful experience of putting the other projects to sleep. Our engineers tested their new design methodologies and validation processes; our manufacturing teams built, tested, and shipped a product; and our sales and support teams were learning about the latest technologies and reengaging with cus-tomers to hear about what they wanted.

Communicating is one of the most important tools in recovering from mistakes. When you tell someone, be it a designer, a customer, or the CEO of the company, "Look, we've got a problem. Here's what it is, here's why it happened, and here's how we're going to fix it," you diffuse the fear of the unknown and focus on the solution. Because we laid out our plan to correct the problem to our customers and shareholders in a clear, straightforward manner, we never lost their trust. We went to each customer affected by the notebook situation and made it right. We said, "We're bringing out a new line. Here's our phased strategy and our service and support plan. Here's why you shouldn't be nervous about doing business with us."

People were genuinely blown away by that. Not because it was rocket science, but because few companies in our industry and in others actually communicate with customers that directly. What we were saying to our customers was, "You're not a customer for just one transaction. You're a customer for life."

The notebook problem illustrated the distinct advantage that the direct model provides to our customers. Dell's relationship with our customers is based on the fact that they can rely on us — not just for one product or in one place but across all product lines and geographic regions. There's no question about who's accountable if there's a product problem, and no question about who's responsible for fixing it. Because of the direct model, we were able to contact our customers quickly and directly, and as a result, recover from the problem fast.

The notebook problem also illustrated how we utilize the direct model within the company. We communicated our three-step strategy as clearly to our people as to our customers and shareholders. When it came to the notebook group, we hung in there together and focused our energies on the one product we had a shot at: the Latitude. Looking back, it was, like the cash crisis, something of a liberating experience, as it forced us to focus fully on one project rather than on too many. With our marching orders in place, everyone knew what they had to do to make Latitude a success.

DAZZLE AND DELIVER

One of the keys to dazzling and delivering on the Latitude was the lithium ion battery.

In January 1993, soon after we had launched Dell in Japan, I met with the folks at Sony. We were talking about monitors and optical drives and CD-ROM drives and all sorts of multimedia technologies that Sony had developed when, toward the end of the meeting, a young Japanese man ran right up to me and said, "Mr. Dell, Mr. Dell, please wait one minute. I'm from the energy power systems group and I need to talk to you."

"Energy power systems?" I thought. "Is this guy going to try to sell me a power plant?"

Still, I was intrigued, so I stayed and listened to what he had to say. He started showing me chart after chart describing the performance of a new battery technology called lithium ion. Suddenly I realized his goal: to sell lithium ion batteries to Dell for our *notebooks*.

Anyone who's ever used a notebook computer will tell you that at the top of her wish list is a long-life battery. Back in 1993, the batteries found in most notebooks ran out after two hours. According to the Sony engineer's performance charts, lithium ion batteries had the potential to last twice as long.

If this was true, I wanted to put lithium ion batteries in every notebook computer we made.

A lithium ion battery has a greater power-to-weight density than a conventional nickel hydride battery. You could save half a pound and gain 50 percent more battery life with lithium ion, not to mention the option of putting intelligence into the battery pack for better power management, which would further extend the life of the battery. Sony had plans to use lithium ion technology in cellular phones and Camcorders that didn't consume anywhere near the power that a notebook computer does. They had never built a battery with the cell size we wanted and the number of cells in a battery pack that we needed, and they saw notebooks as a tremendous opportunity to move into a new market.

Lithium ion became a breakthrough technology.

As easy a decision as this might seem, in retrospect, lithium ion was a brand new technology, and therefore a risk. Because we couldn't support both lithium ion and nickel hydride designs in our system, we had to choose one or the other. And even though the people at Sony kept coming back with the right answers to our questions, no one really knew how lithium ion would hold up. It was a clear differentiator, that was for sure. Lithium ion was so new, no one else was even manufacturing it. With all our demand, Sony wouldn't have enough left over to sell to anyone else. And it would take a competitor at least a year to even get access to the technology. Meanwhile, if all went well, our products would have a tremendous advantage in battery life and size-to-weight.

The Latitude XP with lithium ion battery was introduced in August 1994. To launch it, we invited about fifty industry analysts and reporters on a cross-country flight. We met them at New York's John F. Kennedy Airport, gave each a Latitude XP fully loaded with word-processing software, and flew them nonstop to Los Angeles. By the time the plane landed five and a half hours later, the Latitude XP had broken every record for battery life. Demand for Latitude drove notebook sales from 2 percent of system revenue in the first quarter of fiscal year 1995 to 14 percent by the fourth quarter.

Fortunately, notebooks were now contributing to our growth. But we knew there was even more opportunity ahead.

UNDERPROMISE AND OVERDELIVER

Survival implants a thorough understanding of the ways in which a business earns and spends the money that allows it to open its doors each day. I distinctly remember a period in 1993 when we concluded that *any* additional growth wouldn't have helped us because we didn't really have an adequate understanding of the economics within each of our businesses. It was an awkward phase in our company's history because it was completely different from anything we had ever experienced before.

But it was a learning experience that we could not have done without. We had to grow out of the start-up mentality in order to figure out what to focus on before we could take on new challenges. Instead of pushing the accelerator toward greater growth, we had to hit the brakes before we got too far ahead of ourselves. We had to identify those opportunities that made the most of our strengths and go after only the best ones, rather than trying to go after every opportunity we saw. We had to pace our investments to match our progress, and to hold ourselves to a level of growth that would ensure that we could meet our commitments to our customers, employees, and shareholders. This painful period helped to reinforce the Dell philosophy of "underpromise and overdeliver."

After our losing quarter, we were back in the black faster than most had expected. And then, at the end of 1993, *Upside* magazine named me "Turnaround CEO of the Year."

"Thanks," I thought. "I hope I don't ever win that award again."

Someone once said that the difference between Dell and other companies is that while all companies make mistakes, Dell never makes the same mistake twice. We've always seen mistakes as learning opportunities. The key is to learn well from the mistakes that you make so that you don't repeat them. In our case, learning took the form of some notable public missteps—or, as we sometimes joke, learning opportunities of massive proportions. Fortunately, the lessons we learned helped us identify and implement the practices that gave us a secure foundation for future growth.

NARROWING OUR FOCUS

THERE'S NOTHING QUITE LIKE THE EXPERIENCE we had in 1993 to teach the importance of focus. Growing a company much faster than the industry is growing is great, but when your company grows by as much as 127 percent *in one year*, you can quickly outstrip your ability to manage it effectively. Our problem was not that Dell was in serious decline or that our customers didn't want to buy our products. Quite the opposite, we learned that it was possible to grow too quickly. The problem was that we had been overenthusiastically pursuing every opportunity that presented itself. We needed to learn that not only did we not have to jump at each and every one, as we once did—but that we couldn't and shouldn't, for our overall well-being.

Through our cash-flow crisis and P&L initiative, we began to realize that it's as important to figure out what you're *not* going to do as it is to know what you *are* going to do.

Every year since then, we define several "big, hairy audacious goals"*—key company priorities—based, of course, on liquidity, profitability, and growth. These are the main objectives we focus on for the coming year. We sequence them according to the size of the opportunity and our ability to achieve them. In '93, when we were first learning this very important lesson, we had to take each goal slowly, gradually. And our goals back then were focused on infrastructure as much as market opportunity: build systems and processes; hire, retain, and develop talented people; and build product leadership in notebooks and servers.

Instead of leaping into the abyss of opportunity, as we always had, we had to put one foot in front of the other, in an attempt to grow, yes, but grow deliberately. For a while, we had to channel all our creative energy *not* into creating new things but into enhancing the things we had already created and helping them reach their full potential. We had always been prolific with new ideas; now we needed a more disciplined way of prioritizing all those opportunities. This was a huge adjustment not only for me but for others in the company. We carefully weighed the best new ideas against what else we had on our collective plate, to identify what their real upside would be, in terms of creating value for our customers and shareholders. And then we had to gauge whether or not the opportunity was worth it.

We had to learn the basic steps that most companies, which grow and mature more slowly, learn when they are much smaller in size. We were moving in the right direction with our emphasis on liquidity, profitability, and growth. But we were also challenged by a cultural issue.

We had created an atmosphere in which we were all focused on growth; it was not uncommon to find people in meetings waving

---

*A wonderful phrase for stretch goals or big priorities, coined by James C. Collins and Jerry Porras in their seminal work, *Built to Last*.

huge foam-rubber index fingers and chanting "Tier One," indicating our drive to become one of the top three computer vendors in the world. We had to shift our focus away from an external orientation to one that strengthened our company internally.

For us, growing up meant figuring out a way to combine our signature informal, entrepreneurial style and "want-to" attitude with the "can-do" capabilities that would allow us to develop as a company. It meant incorporating into our everyday structure the valuable lessons we'd begun to learn using P&Ls. It meant focusing our employees to think in terms of shareholder value. It meant respecting the three golden rules at Dell: 1) Disdain inventory, 2) Always listen to the customer, and 3) Never sell indirect.

It sounds simple, I know, but some of the best practices are often the simplest. And even the simple practices take time to institute.

WHY FACTS ARE YOUR FRIEND

We had just gone from a period where everything had been working really well to a period where everything simply wasn't. When things are good, it's counterintuitive to ask, "What's working—and why?" It's also much harder to establish a successful cause-and-effect relationship than it is to pin a problem to a cause. Yet that's exactly what we needed to do to become one of the most profitable companies in the world.

It was clear that in 1993 we didn't have the information we needed to run our business. We didn't fully understand the relationship between costs, revenues, and profits within the different parts of our business. There were internal disagreements about which businesses were worthwhile and which were not. We were making decisions based on emotions and opinions.

In leadership, it's important to be intuitive, but not at the expense of facts. Without the right data to back it up, emotion-based decision-making during difficult times will inevitably lead a company into greater danger. That's precisely what was happening to us.

There's a very easy way to test whether you're making decisions based on emotions. When you come across data that are strikingly different from what you previously thought, how long does it take for you to shift your thinking? Do you deny the data and say, "Well, I don't believe this?"

The longer it takes to accept new data, the more you're relying on your emotions.

Based upon what we'd just been through, we clearly could no longer afford to continue operating in the absence of facts. We needed a complete and rapid adjustment in mind-set.

GAINING PERIPHERAL VISION

I've always tried to surround myself with the best talent I could find. When you're the leader of a company, be it large or small, you can't do everything yourself. In fact, you can't do much of *anything* by yourself. The more talented people you have to help you, the better off you and the company will be. One of the challenges you face as a company grows is that you tend to get a little too close to your own strengths and weaknesses, and it's hard to be objective. I've heard this referred to as "believing your own press," but I prefer to think of it as "breathing your own exhaust."

It doesn't sound healthy—because it isn't.

An outsider's point of view can be especially useful when you're tangled up in a problem that's obscured by a lack of clear facts. A fresh set of eyes distanced from the day-to-day reality can often provide an objective perspective.

In August of 1993, in the middle of one of the most challenging periods in our company's history, I outlined a blueprint for the company's recovery for our Board of Directors. One of the items on the list was to get some outside help.

We knew by now that there were areas where we were making money, and areas where we weren't. But we hadn't yet evolved enough to know exactly where, company-wide, nor did we know the magnitude of this disparity. So we called Bain & Company, with whom we'd successfully worked before, to help us out again. It was at this point that Kevin Rollins, the lead partner at Bain for Dell, became an integral part of our executive team.

In keeping with our P&L plan, we worked with Bain to further dissect the business into its component parts. Based on this, we were able to develop a set of metrics that determined which business units were succeeding and which weren't. We could compare one group's metrics to another's, identify performance opportunities, and accelerate growth in areas that made money. Once we determined which groups weren't performing as well, we could study the groups that were, and make an informed decision about if and how we could improve the lower performers—and if not, whether to cut our losses and close them down.

It was a wonderfully efficient, liberating framework.

In fact, it was all about assigning responsibility and accountability to the managers of these businesses. And while one might wonder whether this was embraced by the managers, the truth is, it generally was. Indeed, there were some managers within Dell who resisted the use of facts and data in daily decision-making, and as painful as it was for all of us, they eventually left. But for the most part, people were very energized by the change. There was something of a catharsis in the company culture as the old way of thinking gave way to the new. This was the first time we had really made a meaningful cultural adjustment, and we carefully communicated what this meant for the company's future to our employees, customers, and shareholders. It was met with an overwhelmingly positive response because of the clarity of vision it afforded. "Facts are your friend" soon became a common phrase at Dell. We were still the same company—marked by the same Dell drive and spirit—but we were better armed to make important decisions, which was the focus we needed to forge ahead and continue to succeed.

Beyond being able to measure what we were doing well and what was lacking, we learned something more that affected the very structure of our organization. We realized that, because Dell's cost structure was so heavily driven by "touch the customer" activities, not only did our P&Ls have to be centered around customer-oriented activities, but our *organization* should be as well. We weren't, in fact, one big business. We were an amalgam of several different businesses. In order to best serve each distinct business, we would have to disaggregate the whole and change the fundamental structure of the company.

This was no small feat.

BECOMING FUNCTIONAL AGAIN

Like many companies, we had organized our business around functions, such as product development, finance, sales and marketing, and manufacturing. But what happened was that, as a functional organization, we had grown beyond those self-imposed boundaries to the point that the functions had begun to take on a life of their own. As we grew larger, it became increasingly more difficult to work as an integrated team. Instead of moving coherently forward in a unified way, the functional divisions had given way to a loosely linked collection of fiefdoms — or "silos," as we called them.

Without a clear vision of how each division contributed to the company's overall well-being, the managers of the different functional groups had begun barricading themselves in their own silos and had begun to think primarily of promoting and protecting their own group's interests. In the thick of our growth, our team had lost sight of our fundamental values: serving the interests of the customer, the shareholder, and the company as a whole. The information systems group, for example, would say, "We're the information systems group and our job is to create information systems," rather than, "We're the information systems group and our job is to facilitate the flow of information to our employees, customers, and shareholders." This kind of compartmentalization makes it nearly impossible to forge the necessary links among people so that they will talk to one another and work together toward a common set of goals. Instead of having a company where everyone takes responsibility for their actions and contemplates and understands how those actions affect other parts of the company, you have an environment in which people are saying, "That's not *my* job. That's his job."

As we grew from a $900 million company to a $3 billion company, it became clear that this functional structure simply wasn't working for us. It became difficult to identify, much less accomplish, our company-wide objectives.

These days, I sometimes joke about how my high school didn't teach any courses in how to manage a $3 billion company. But it wasn't funny at the time. We needed to change and I needed additional help.

SEARCHING FOR BILLION-DOLLAR MANAGEMENT

A company's success should always be defined by its strategy and its ideas—and it should not be limited by the abilities of the people who are running it. As a manager and CEO, I was aware of my strengths and my weaknesses.

Over the years, I had brought in Lee Walker as president. When he left in 1989, I shared those responsibilities with some of our other managers. I had hired Tom Meredith when I knew we needed to strengthen our financial expertise, and hired Bain when it was time for an objective look at our strategy.

I knew that aside from being smart, we had also been lucky. Half of all start-ups in America get wiped out by the kind of crises we had just weathered, and I knew this was especially true of technology companies. I didn't have to look very far for examples of companies that had skyrocketed onto the scene and then fizzled out—or whose founders had been ousted. There were plenty of examples in the computer industry alone: Steve Jobs at Apple in 1985, Ken Olsen at

Digital Equipment Corporation, and Rod Canion at Compaq.

We had outgrown the management that had worked when we were a multimillion-dollar company. Now that we were a multi*billion*-dollar company, we needed billion-dollar management.

By the end of 1993, it was apparent that there was too much for me to handle on my own. There were customers whom I wanted to spend time with. There were management meetings and operations reviews I wanted to attend. There were speeches I wanted to make. I wanted to have the time to spend with our employees, in order to better understand their challenges and provide whatever help or insight I could on how they might improve different parts of the business.

I wanted to grow and develop myself. And I wanted to maintain a healthy balance in my life, and spend time with my young and rapidly growing family.

When you're trying to grow a new business, you really need the experience of others who have been there and can help you anticipate and plan for things you might never have thought of. And of course, the challenge in building a business like ours is that you're constantly confronted with situations no one has ever seen before, so you need to strike a balance between experience, intellect, and adaptability. Someone with tremendous experience might be able to tell you exactly what has happened in situations past, but as they say in financial prospectuses, past performance is not necessarily an indicator of future performance.

The best combination is a management team that has both experience and intellect, and can respond quickly in a dynamic and constantly changing industry. This is one of the reasons why, if you look at our executive team today, you will see people from very different backgrounds and experience.

I met Mort Topfer in January 1994. Mort's background was in the communications industry rather than the computer industry—he was an executive vice president at Motorola and headed their land mobile and data systems products. But the type of products and product cycles he had dealt with were not drastically different from ours. Also, the business Mort was running was about the size of Dell at that time. Equally important was the fact that Mort, among his many experiences, had already been through the transformation from a functional organization to an organization of general managers. When I had to decide whether to brave this journey alone or bring in someone who had already been there, someone who could point out the pitfalls and help us get past them, there was no question in my mind.

Dell needed Mort.

Mort and I met many, many times, as this was a decision—and a relationship—that neither of us took lightly. We spent a great deal of time getting to know each other, comparing philosophies, sharing history, and strategizing about where the company was, and where it was going. If someone was going to join the company at that level, it was important to both of us that it be a perfect fit. Mort joined us as vice-chairman in May 1994.

SHARING POWER

For any company to succeed, it's critical for top management to share power successfully. You have to be focused on achieving goals for the organization, not on accumulating power for yourself. Hoarding power does not translate into success for shareholders and customers; pursuing the goals of the company does. You also need to respect one another, and communicate so constantly that you're practically of one mind on the most important topics and issues that face the company.

In our case, the opportunities and challenges were so dramatic that it was never tough to figure out who would do what; there was always much more to be done than either of us could do. I focused primarily on products, technology, and overall strategy while Mort focused on operations, sales, and marketing. I worked on customer relationships and the external things, like giving speeches and meeting the press and analysts. Mort concentrated on the budget and the day-to-day responsibilities of running the company.

Ultimately, the responsibilities outlined in this division of labor meshed. Customer relationships, for example, were inextricably bound to sales, so there was—and is—much give-and-take. Sometimes we even trade schedules. The key to our success has been that we immediately established a fluidity and consistency of communication that has affected the company on every level.

PLAN OR DIE

Planning is one of those areas where experience counts as much as intellect. When you're trying to grow a new business, it's hard to anticipate the ups and downs of business cycles that you've actually never experienced before.

It seems a little naive in retrospect, but before Mort, we didn't do a heck of a lot of detailed long-range planning. We didn't have to when we were "young," and by the time we should have, we were already working hard to meet our short-term goals. What was great about 1994 was that we were starting fresh. We had the elements of a strong management team, which, for the first time in the company's history, allowed us to look beyond the twelve-month framework and study the true potential of the business long-term.

Mort helped identify the need to insert more discipline into our planning process. He helped us understand that planning was not a quarterly event, but an ongoing process. And it was not just an internal initiative, but a system that involves every part of the supply chain, customer and employee base. Given our new focus on accountability, this made perfect sense.

For the first time, we put together a robust three-year plan for the entire company. This planning process revealed a number of key issues about the organization, its facilities, infrastructure, and growth opportunities. We looked at our market share country by country and product by product, and examined its growth potential. We carefully analyzed our competitors' cost structures, and if they were winning against us, examined them closely in order to understand why. This intense review led us to conclude, for example, that to gain share in the home and small business market, we would have to change our cost structure over the next several years to price our products more aggressively. And at the same time, we needed to evolve our product design strategy for this segment to focus on much higher levels of power and performance.

We figured out where we could afford to make new investments, identified where we might be more aggressive, and determined where caution was warranted. And we communicated these opportunities to the entire company, which responded as enthusiastically as it had earlier to our P&L and data initiatives. People found the change of focus from the next quarter or the next half year to two, three, and five years into the future motivating and encouraging. It allowed them to be creative in thinking about what we had to do to achieve our goals. Since one of our stretch goals was to turn our $3 billion business into a $10 billion business in three years, it got them pretty excited to be working at Dell.*

There was no area of the company that wasn't affected by this new approach of integrated planning. We looked at our head count and realized that we'd need to hire a huge number of people over the next several years, and that we'd need to develop a large team of senior managers to run the new businesses that we could create. We looked at our supplier relationships and concluded that to meet our goals, we would need tremendous unit volumes of supply—three to five

---

*At the time, we thought this a somewhat ambitious but achievable plan. As it turned out, we significantly overachieved our target, hitting $12.2 billion in three years.

times the amount we had in 1994. We didn't want to end up maxing out our suppliers' output or using up the world's supply of flat-panel displays, so we asked our procurement teams to develop three-year plans with each of our suppliers.

We looked at our sales process and knew that if we were to meet our goal of achieving 30 percent of our sales in notebooks, we would need a commensurate capacity in our manufacturing plants, as well as the sales force and the component supply to make this all happen.

Strategically, at least, we were back on track—and it felt good.

The key to creating a plan that's challenging but achievable is having enough data. The more data we extract about the different businesses within our company, the better we are able to see the strengths and the opportunities for improvement. To say that we have become a data-driven company is almost an understatement. Data is *the* engine that keeps us on track. It's hard to believe, looking back, but we went from one big hunk of business to more than four thousand different types of analyses that we now apply when examining our P&Ls.

Of course, you don't ever really know whether you've come up with the right plan until much later—when either it works or it doesn't. What is the right plan? It's the one that helps you identify what you need to do to ensure success. It's the one that rallies your employees around a few common goals—and motivates them to achieve them. It's one that involves your customers' goals and your suppliers' goals and brings them all together in a unified focus.

That's an invaluable lesson for any growing company.

DIALING UP, DELIBERATELY

PLANNING IS NOTHING WITHOUT execution. Yet we learned that lesson the old-fashioned way, too—by making mistakes. Back in the early 1990s, if you asked a number of different product managers at Dell how their products got to market, you'd get a handful of different answers. Juggling these different development processes worked pretty well in getting new products out quickly when we were small. But as the volume and diversity of our products magnified, it became clear that we had to standardize this process.

So we hired a firm that specialized in helping high-tech companies organize their product development processes, and we worked with them to create a unique phase review process that best suited the needs of our business. This was not a quick-fix solution; it actually took a couple of years to totally take hold, because you can't just disrupt the flow of ongoing projects. But it was exactly the right kind of planning discipline that we needed as we grew from thousands to tens of thousands of people and from a handful to hundreds of products. This process created the common language and an agreement across the organization about how projects would be developed and launched. And because it has been so instrumental to our success, the phase review process is worth describing in detail.

We start with a business contract, which is an agreement among all parts of the organization concerning the product we intend to deliver: what it is, and how it's supposed to perform in the market. Each phase has its own criteria for achievement. From the beginning, everyone signs on: from design and manufacturing to finance, sales, and services and support. The phase review process becomes a robust planning architecture for the development of each product because it fosters team responsibility and accountability.

It also serves as a template for a financial planning process that is now central to the way the company develops its budgets and sets metrics and goals for the organization. That process involves a combination of looking at the potential of the market and evaluating our opportunity, based on our capabilities and the resources required. Because we glean data on all customers and products from countries around the world, we know what we ought to be able to achieve in terms of market penetration, sales force productivity, and other aspects of our business. The planning process is both bottom-up, in terms of what the individual business thinks it can achieve, and top-down, in terms of what management thinks it could and should achieve. Both are very, very important.

We've discovered that having a common language and effectively sharing common goals actually enhances our organizational structure, which in turn kicks the company into higher gear. In a company that's as large and rapidly growing as ours, you obviously can't have a traditional functional organization, nor a completely decentralized model. The former ends up being a bunch of unconnected groups with unclear accountability; the latter is not a company, it's a mutual fund. You need to maintain functional excellence while injecting business accountability.

To achieve this, we instituted a system of dual reporting with our people. Most senior-level managers of specific functions, such as finance or human resources or legal affairs, share responsibility with managers of specific businesses, such as particular regions or product lines. Our lawyers in Europe, for example, report both to the head of our European business, as well as to our general counsel at our headquarters in Round Rock.

People often say, "there has to be one boss," and "matrix management doesn't work." In fact, dual reporting works very effectively at Dell.

The key is to have overlapping but complete accountability. Managers share, through their formal performance reviews, responsibility for the success of the people they jointly manage, and for the ultimate business outcome—even for the part that is technically within the other person's functional area.

It's really a system of checks and balances. Sharing responsibility results in a joint accountability and encourages collaboration, but it also results in sharing different perspectives and ideas across a company.

Dual reporting creates a tremendous amount of energy and enthusiasm throughout the organization. And we channel that energy into action, producing growth through a process called "segmentation."

DIVIDE AND CONQUER

When you've got a huge market opportunity facing you, the only way to handle it is to divide and conquer. That's the basis behind our concept of segmentation. It ensures that as we grow, we are able to serve each individual customer more effectively, and it has become the organizing philosophy of our company.

Most companies segment by product. We decided also to segment by customer. We believe that a customer's unique needs and behaviors more closely determine what products and services we should develop for them. And because Dell sells directly to our customers, understanding the unique needs of each customer allows us to address them better.

Look at it this way: If you organize a company like ours around products, you have to assume that the people who are running the business know everything there is to know about the customers who buy those products—not just here, but everywhere in the world. That's a pretty big assumption. Believing that an organization that is focused on a particular type of customer in a particular region of the world knows everything about those customers is a lot easier to fathom.

From the very beginning of the company's existence, we realized that we had different kinds of customers. Take, for example, our large corporate customers and consumers. Each group buys different products, has different cost structures associated with servicing those products, and even uses different sales models. The sales model for large customers utilizes face-to-face contacts and the telephone, as well as the Internet. Consumers and small businesses are served primarily with a telephone- and Internet-based sales model. Segmentation initially started as a sales concept to most effectively meet the needs of different groups of customers. We created different sales organizations that specialized in understanding the needs of these customers, and as we grew, we split those customer segments into large and medium-sized companies, educational institutions and government organizations, and small businesses and consumers.

This idea goes beyond the concept of simple demographics—that is, what age group you are in or what the size of your business is. We segment according to customer needs *and* behaviors; *how* a customer uses our product is as important to its features as what they will use it for.

We learned how powerful this idea was with some experimentation in the early 90s, when we designed a series of products that we called "PCs for People." Each of the five products in the series was designed for a particular type of computer user, from the "techno-teamer," who uses a networked computer for work that is largely job- and team-oriented, to the "techno-critical," who is more frequently an independent operator, relying on his computer for more sophisticated tasks such as computer-aided design.

We also believe that segmenting by customer is the right way to operate, because the majority of the company's costs are aligned toward serving the customer. Segmentation by customer means that the responsibility for satisfying the customer is ultimately shared throughout the company. You might be responsible for selling computer systems to banks or large companies in the United Kingdom, but you'd also have someone on your team who knows all about servers and storage products—and who looks at technical product requirements in a customer context.

But while we've organized our company around customer groups, we don't only look at the performance of customer P&Ls. We also look at product profits and losses. While we want to understand how we're doing in Germany with consumers and large companies, we also want to know how we're doing in each country around the world with particular products. In other words, we've got to walk and chew gum at the same time.

Segmentation is not a new idea. But like many things at Dell, it has worked so well for us because we do it differently.

SEGMENTING BEYOND SALES

What started as a sales concept to maximize market opportunities soon evolved into a series of complete business units, each with its own sales, service, finance, IT, technical support, and manufacturing arms. It really makes sense for our business. Our direct connection to our customers enables us to understand the different needs of different customers. Segmentation takes the closed feedback loop and makes it even smaller and more intimate. It refines our relationship with our customers.

As we deepened our understanding of each customer segment, we also developed a better understanding of how to measure its financial opportunity. One of the great things about segmentation is that it has allowed us to see the growth rates, profitability, service level performance, and market share in each unique segment, and adjust our activities accordingly. We found that we had some businesses that were earning a very high profit but were not growing very fast. We found other businesses that were growing very fast but not earning much of a profit. We didn't want either. We wanted businesses that were growing quickly *and* earning a reasonable profit.

Segmentation also enabled us to measure the efficiency of these businesses in terms of their asset use. This meant we could evaluate our return on invested capital in each segment, compare it with other segments, and target what the performance of each should be. It became a great way to identify what needed to happen for us to reach our full potential in each business.

We took the concepts we had begun to explore in our PCs for People program to a more sophisticated level, segmenting our product lines to align with different customer groups. We started with one basic product line of desktop PCs. In 1994, we dedicated the OptiPlex line to corporate environments, which placed a high value on networking and the consistency of the platform, and created the Dimension line for technologically sophisticated individuals and small businesses. We reentered the notebook computer market in February 1994, with the 486-based Latitude family, which has since segmented into the Latitude line for corporate users and the Inspiron line for home and small business users.

As we continue to grow, we constantly look at and segment our business to better understand all the available opportunities. For example, we never would have developed our market for midsized customers had we stuck with our original configuration of large and small customer groups. But we realized that there was a market somewhere in between that had its own special needs. Recently, we split the education segment in the United States into the K-12 and higher education markets, because each segment has its own different product and and service requirements.

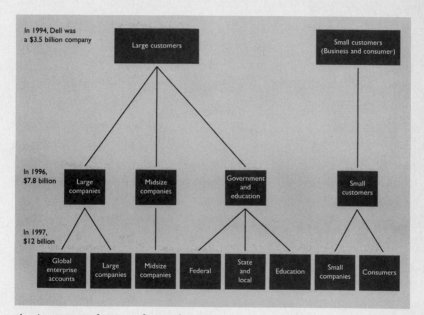

An important element of virtual integration with customers is segmentation. The finer the segmentation, the better able Dell is to forecast what our customers are going to need and when. We then coordinate the flow of that strategic information all the way back to our suppliers, effectively substituting information for inventory.

Customers can't help noticing the difference between what a traditional product-focused organization offers and what we can provide.

In a word, it's service. Whether it's anticipating their technology needs or supporting them with fast, reliable delivery and on-site service, we've been able to create a feeling of personalization—of a relationship—that comes with buying a PC from Dell. And while some have expressed concern that as we grow, we'll lose touch with them, we have found that the opposite happens. Each time we segment, we learn a little more about a customer's unique set of needs. It's our goal to know our customers' needs as well as or better than they do.

Segmentation offers a solution to the fundamental issue that has challenged Dell since the very beginning: how to sustain our growth as we got bigger. You can grow small companies quickly, but it becomes increasingly more difficult to sustain a high rate of growth in a large corporation. Segmentation allows us to scale our business very rapidly, because every time we determine that there is sufficient momentum to segment a unique customer group, we'll break it off, give it its own organization team, and let it act as a small company.

Together, our segments enable us, as a large company, to post the growth rates of a small one.

RETAIL: FIRST IN, FIRST OUT

Segmentation also led us to reemphasize the value of putting our resources only—and exactly—where they make the most sense. Our period of overexpansion taught us the importance of determining where we wanted to deliver value. But after segmenting the organization in such a logical and organic way, Mort and I realized we had left one rather large stone unturned.

Even though we were busy focusing on the direct model, we were still selling computers in retail markets. If there was ever an area worth running a P&L on, retail was it.

It's important to note that at that time—1994—the retail business was booming at a 20 percent growth rate. While all of our competitors were getting more deeply into retail, I had begun wondering if we should pull out. We had been in it for about four years, and we were selling through five mass-market chains, including electronics super-stores like CompUSA and Circuit City.

Mort and I took a hard look at the data available to us, and realized an amazing thing. Even though we were successfully selling PCs via the retail channels, we weren't actually making any money—nor, did we believe, was our competition! We looked closely at how we could change the product mix or lower costs to improve profitability. Still, we couldn't find the profit core, so we decided to take a hard line. We put our retail group on notice and asked them to justify their business. One of the last-gasp efforts they made was to expand our retail PC sales beyond the superstores and clubs into places like Wal-Mart and Best Buy. But even that didn't help.

Later that same year, we decided to exit the retail operation, mere months after we'd announced with great fanfare that we'd be selling in Wal-Mart. Fortunately, retail had represented only a small per-centage of our sales. I knew in my gut it was the right thing to do, but I also had the data to back up my suspicions. Others didn't see it quite that way. Virtually every news story on the subject said that Dell was going to severely limit its growth by getting out of retail. Industry ana-lysts said it was a mistake; they, too, predicted that our growth would slow. And despite the many improvements we were making struc-turally within the organization, there was still doubt among some of our people internally as to whether retail was superior to dealing direct in the consumer market.

The benefit of exiting retail was not just the change in our finan-cial condition, because that was relatively minor. The real value was that it forced all of our people to focus 100 percent on the direct model. That singlemindedness was a powerful unifying force. Before, we had product people working to support both the indirect and the direct channels, and doing half a job on each. We had manufacturing people wondering whether to build a plant that supplied the retail channel, which demanded different specifications, or a plant for the direct model. We had sales representatives dealing with service and support conflicts from customers that we had created ourselves by trying to be both direct and indirect at the same time.

The retail experience had clearly unsettled some of our people. Whereas before we had always dealt fully and directly with all of our customers, some of our employees felt distanced by our foray into retail and missed the energy they derived from direct relationships.

Soon after we got out of retail, we began talking about the direct model in a very pure sense, and our people rallied around this rebirth. They were grateful for the clarity that getting into—and out of—retail had afforded. We had reaffirmed that dealing direct was one of our key differentiators, in terms of delivering high-quality systems quickly, efficiently, and with great service. And we learned that it was the key to securing our future as a leader in the industry.

We had found the truth, and it was direct.

THE DIRECT MODEL, VERSION 1.1

Turning the business around involved more than segmenting and pulling out of retail. It also meant maximizing every strength we had in order to boost our profit margins. In reexamining the direct model, we realized that inventory management was not just a core strength; it could be an incredible opportunity for us, and one that had not yet been discovered by any of our competitors.

In Version 1.0 of the direct model, we eliminated the reseller, thereby eliminating the markup and the cost of maintaining a store. In Version 1.1, we went one step further to reduce inventory inefficiencies.

Traditionally, a long chain of partners was involved in getting a product to the customer. Let's say you have a factory building a PC we'll call model #4000. The system is then sent to the distributor, which sends it to the warehouse, which sends it to the dealer, who eventually pushes it on to the consumer by advertising, "I've got model #4000. Come and buy it." If the consumer says, "But I want model #8000," the dealer replies, "Sorry, I only have model #4000." Meanwhile, the factory keeps building model #4000s and pushing the inventory into the channel.

The result is a glut of model #4000s that nobody wants. Inevitably, someone ends up with too much inventory, and you see big price corrections. The retailer can't sell it at the suggested retail price, so the manufacturer loses money on price protection (a practice common in our industry of compensating dealers for reductions in suggested selling price).

Companies with long, multistep distribution systems will often fill their distribution channels with products in an attempt to clear out older technologies or meet their financial targets. This dangerous and inefficient practice is called "channel stuffing." Worst of all, the customer ends up paying for it by purchasing systems that are already out of date.

Because we were building directly to fill our customers' orders, we didn't have finished goods inventory devaluing on a daily basis. Because we aligned our suppliers to deliver components as we used them, we were able to minimize raw material inventory. Reductions in component costs could be passed on to our customers quickly, which made them happier and improved our competitive advantage. It also allowed us to deliver the latest technology to our customers faster than our competitors.

The direct model turns conventional manufacturing inside out. Conventional manufacturing dictates that you should always have a stockpile of raw materials, because if you run out, your plant can't keep going. But if you don't know what you need to build because of dramatic changes in demand, you run the risk of ending up with terrific amounts of excess and obsolete inventory. That is not the goal.

The concept behind the direct model has nothing to do with stockpiling and everything to do with information.

The quality of your information is inversely proportional to the amount of assets required, in this case excess inventory. With less information about customer needs, you need massive amounts of inventory. So, if you have great information—that is, you know exactly what people want and how much—you need that much less inventory.

Less inventory, of course, corresponds to less inventory depreciation. In the computer industry, component prices are always falling as suppliers introduce faster chips, bigger disk drives, and modems with ever-greater bandwidth. Let's say that Dell has six days of inventory. Compare that to an indirect competitor who has twenty-five days of inventory with another thirty in their distribution channel. That's a difference of forty-nine days, and in forty-nine days, the cost of materials will decline about 6 percent.

Then there's the threat of getting stuck with obsolete inventory if you're caught in a transition to a next-generation product, as we were with those memory chips in 1989. As the product approaches the end of its life, the manufacturer has to worry about whether it has too much in the channel and whether a competitor will dump products, destroying profit margins for everyone. This is a perpetual problem in the computer industry, but with the direct model, we have virtually eliminated it. We know when our customers are ready to move on technologically, and we can get out of the market before its most precarious time. We don't have to subsidize our losses by charging higher prices for other products.

And ultimately, our customer wins.

Optimal inventory management really starts with the design process. You want to design the product so that the entire product supply chain, as well as the manufacturing process, is oriented not just for speed but for what we call velocity. Speed means being fast in the first place. Velocity means squeezing time out of every step in the process.

Inventory velocity has become a passion for us. To achieve maximum velocity, you have to design your products in a way that covers the largest part of the market with the fewest number of parts. For example, you don't need nine different disk drives when you can serve 98 percent of the market with only four. We also learned to take into account the variability of low- and high-cost components. Systems were reconfigured to allow for a greater variety of low-cost parts and a limited variety of expensive parts. The goal was to decrease the number of components to manage, which increased the velocity, which decreased the risk of inventory depreciation, which increased the overall health of our business system.

We were also able to reduce inventory well below the levels anyone thought possible by constantly challenging and surprising ourselves with the results. We had our internal skeptics when we first started pushing for ever-lower levels of inventory. I remember the head of our procurement group telling me that this was like "flying low to the ground at 800 knots." He was worried that we wouldn't see the trees.

In 1993, we had $2.9 billion in sales and $220 million in inventory. Four years later, we posted $12.3 billion in sales and had inventory of $233 million. We're now down to six days of inventory and we're starting to measure it in hours instead of days.

Once you reduce your inventory while maintaining your growth rate, a significant amount of risk comes from the transition from one generation of product to the next. Without traditional stockpiles of inventory, it is critical to precisely time the discontinuance of the older product line with the ramp-up in customer demand for the newer one. Since we were introducing new products all the time, it became imperative to avoid the huge drag effect from mistakes made during transitions. E&O—short for "excess and obsolete"—became taboo at Dell. We would debate about whether our E&O was 30 or 50 cents per PC. Since anything less than $20 per PC is not bad, when you're down in the cents range, you're approaching stellar performance.

In effect, we got stronger with each transition and more competitive with each turn of the crank. We were increasing our productivity and improving our cash flow in a broader range of products in larger and larger markets. Unlike that period in 1993, when every day the news got a little worse, now, finally, every day the news was better and better.

At last, we were on the right path, and we were taking the business to a totally new level.

SCALING WITH SERVERS

By the mid-1990s, everything was coming together. Thanks to segmentation, we were scaling globally. In 1995, sales in the United States, Canada, and Latin America grew nearly three times faster than the market rate. We had offices in fourteen countries in Europe, solidified our position as the second-largest computer company in the United Kingdom, and continued to extend the direct model in France and Germany, posting sales rates well above the average. We expanded our position in the Asia-Pacific/Japan region, offering direct operations in eleven countries and distribution alliances in thirty-seven more. We were building systems and infrastructure and developing a world-class workforce.

But as unbelievable as it sounds, we again realized that we were facing the proposition of grow or die. The industry continued to consolidate, and we had to meet the challenge of extending the Dell brand beyond our strong desktop and notebook franchises.

The next logical step was servers.

Entering the server business was not only a huge opportunity but clearly a competitive necessity. An explosion of networked and internetworked systems was occurring throughout corporations, which meant that our present customers—the techno-savvy, second- or third-time buyers who were our core market—would be looking to make big purchases.

At the same time, the emergence of industry standards for operating systems (Windows NT) and multiprocessor servers meant that Dell could develop its own server systems based on these standards and avoid massive investments in new proprietary technologies that would ultimately become very costly for our customers. It also meant that we did not have to acquire a competitor to enter the server business.

We could profit by offering lower prices through the direct model. We could, in effect, shatter the price premium customers were paying for proprietary server technologies.

The alternative wasn't pretty. Servers were a force literally big enough to change the operating environment. If we ignored them, the market would consolidate around the top three providers—Compaq, IBM, and HP. We would be seen as a bit player, and would lose our standing with technology providers. And our operating margins would start to thin.

Our large competitors also were using excessively high margins in servers to subsidize the less profitable parts of their business, like desktops and notebooks. If we didn't move into servers, we would be greatly exposed to attack in the desktop and notebook market.

We had the opportunity to do with servers what we had originally done with desktops and then notebooks: rapidly build market share by offering higher performance at a lower price, simultaneously forcing our competitors to lower their server prices and collapse their margins to the point where they couldn't afford to subsidize their other product lines. We couldn't afford not to take such an opportunity.

Our strategy was to develop leading entry-level and midrange server products ourselves. Meanwhile, we would build volume and develop our capability to provide higher-end products and services. That meant creating demand through field-based account executives, systems engineers, phone-based direct sales, and alliances with software and services companies. It meant fulfilling demand through our build-to-order model, including integrating systems and software in our factory. It meant earning our customers' loyalty with stellar service and support.

It wasn't going to be easy. In order to become number four, we had set our sights on grabbing 8 percent market share. To do that, we'd need to ship 10,000 units per month in less than two years, up from our current rate of about 1,200 units per month. We would have to double our volume year over year for the next three years. And we'd have to persuade customers that Dell's direct model worked just as well with servers as with desktops and notebooks, something conventional wisdom deemed utterly impossible.

We explained all of this to our Board of Directors in a meeting in March 1996. They supported our approach and agreed that a strong server initiative was of utmost importance to our future.

Now all we had to do was make it happen.

A RISK WELL TAKEN

We went into high gear to communicate to everyone the necessity of achieving our goals in servers. We sent out company-wide "Message from Michael" e-mails, put up posters in high-traffic areas, and talked through the strategy at numerous brown-bag lunches and company get-togethers. We staged a huge event—"The Great Dell Torch Event"—for seven thousand employees in an auditorium in downtown Austin just to drive the point home. Someone dressed up as Server Man, complete with a cloak and tights and a big red "S" on his chest, and went around to all the buildings to get people revved up about attending the event. I opened the evening by running into the auditorium carrying an Olympic-sized torch.

It was a lot of fun, but it also worked in a big way. According to the metrics taken after the event, 98 percent of those who attended understood our server strategy, and their role in propagating it.

We also educated our customers. In virtually every meeting I had or speech I gave, I made a point of telling customers that we had aggressively entered the server market. I told our customers to ask their server vendors to meet Dell's pricing, and that by doing this, they would at least be assured of saving money on current purchases, even if they didn't select a Dell. I also explained that they would benefit by doing this because they would ultimately take away our competitors' ability to cross-subsidize other products in other markets at the customers' expense.

Customers were not only grateful for the tip, but later told us that they were able to save substantial amounts of money on server purchases as a result of our entry into the market. In fact, in our first year with PowerEdge servers, our competitors had to drop their prices about 17 percent.

Following eighteen months of preparation in building the infrastructure needed to support an expanded server business, in 1996 we launched our PowerEdge single- and dual-processor servers at prices that made network computing more affordable for many businesses. Our goal was to have a double-digit market share in the United States by the end of 1998; we achieved that goal in the middle of 1997. By the end of 1997, we had gone from tenth to fourth place worldwide; by the fall of 1998, we had taken the number two position in the U.S., passing IBM and Hewlett-Packard, and achieving a market share of over 19 percent. Perhaps even more significant is the fact that Dell is the only server provider growing substantially faster than the rest of the market.

Once again we proved what others said could not be done: Servers could and would sell through the Dell direct model.

Looking back over the ups and downs leading up to and including our success in servers, it's clear to me that that success could not have happened without a serious adjustment in how we collected and processed information. We slowed our growth just enough to figure out exactly where we wanted to rev it up again. We devised a more efficient way of structuring our profit centers, as well as our actual organization. We got out of retail, which enabled us to focus, expand, and enhance the competitive advantage inherent in the direct model. And we uncovered even more opportunities implicit in dealing direct with customers, from product design to inventory management.

Not until we sat down and studied the economics of our business did we see all of the incredible opportunities that were in front of us.

The biggest one, however, was yet to come.

REVOLUTIONIZING
AN INDUSTRY

I OFTEN WONDER WHAT NEW DEVELOP-
ment will come along and totally change the face of our industry.
You can be sure it will happen, it's just a question of when and what it
is. It can be a new technology, a new operating environment, a new
market, or even a new competitor. The most important question to Dell
is: Will we be able to identify it? Will we be able to take full advantage
of it? How we navigate the inevitable changes in our industry will
define whether Dell is a good company, or a truly great company.

The Internet has been, without question, one of those developments that I knew had the potential to totally alter our industry.

BACK TO THE FUTURE

When I first became interested in computers, one of the first things I
did was set up a bulletin board system to correspond with people

electronically. Anyone in the country who had a modem could call in and exchange messages with me and with other users. These systems—and there were tens of thousands of them—were the precursors to America Online and today's popular use of the Internet.

My own interest in the Internet started in the early 1990s. The really serious "propeller heads" were all talking about an electronic network that could transport information, which was largely concentrated in universities and government systems.

At that time, commerce on the Internet was pretty much restricted to ordering T-shirts. But it immediately struck me that if you could order a T-shirt online, you could order anything—including a computer. And the great thing was, you needed a computer to do this! I couldn't imagine a more powerful creation for extending our business.

Back in the late 1980s, we had talked about developing a system that would enable our customers to order and configure PCs using modems. After thinking about it for a while, we concluded that it would be just too hard and too expensive to do at that time. There were so many different software platforms then (as opposed to a standard platform), requiring many different versions of the program, which we would have to support ourselves.

Things started to change around 1989 when a researcher at CERN, Tim Berners-Lee, created the World Wide Web (WWW), which was the first practical hypertext system that brought a simpler interface between users and the Internet. Then in 1993, public interest in the Internet really took off when Marc Andreesen and others at the University of Illinois at Urbana-Champaign created the Mosaic browser, which touched off a whole new way of using the Internet to share and exchange information. The browser was a natural outgrowth of the electronic bulletin board system but on a much grander scale. Unlike the bulletin board system, which required that the end user create it, the Mosaic browser provided a standardized interface so that the Internet was accessible to any user.

I was enthralled by the concept; I loved the idea of being able to turn on a PC and see what was going on anywhere in the world. As soon as I could get my hands on it, I installed the Mosaic browser on a machine in my house, and would spend tons of time on the Internet every night after my kids had gone to sleep.

The World Wide Web provided a way to link our customers with all the information they needed to buy and manage their computers, and do it in real time. It worked for everyone, no matter what software platform they used. Even better, there was an almost instantaneous alignment with our customer base; the Internet immediately attracted knowledgeable users, to whom Dell primarily sells. We knew that our customers—and potential customers—would be there first.

LAUNCHING *WWW.DELL.COM*

Dell already had a minor presence on the Internet, thanks to our technology support organization. Back in the late 1980s, some of our technical support guys had set up what's known as a File Transfer Protocol, or FTP, site. If you were affiliated with a university or a government organization that was connected to the Internet and you needed a file, you could download it from our FTP server. (We take this for granted nowadays, but back then it was a big deal.)

The FTP site, however, while helping customers, did nothing to enhance the Dell brand. It didn't differentiate us from any of our competitors, many of whom offered the same sort of service. And it did nothing to explore the opportunity that existed for extending the strengths of the direct model.

A site on the World Wide Web, however, promised to do all that—and more.

Companies were, at this time, experimenting on the World Wide Web, but many didn't really know what to do with it. Few had web pages, and those that did generally posted their annual reports, press releases, and marketing information in a static form. Most of the talk about the Internet focused on its use as an information medium, offering a wealth of entertainment and value-added services available to anyone who had a PC and knew about the Internet's many advantages.

However, the demand for commerce was growing as security enhancements were increasingly incorporated into browser and server technology, and a few revenue-generating sites emerged. Almost universally, industry observers predicted a surge in electronic commerce. According to one forecast at the time, business-to-business Internet commerce would be $67 billion annually by the year 2000.*

We realized, at this early stage, that the Internet represented a world of untapped potential—especially for a business like ours. We also knew then that the Internet offered incredible branding opportunities. If we didn't establish an early position as *the* online source for systems and service, one of our competitors would.

In June 1994, we launched *www.dell.com*. It contained technical support information and an e-mail link for support, and was aimed primarily at the savvy users who tended to be early adopters of new technologies. They soon told us that they wanted a way to calculate the cost of different PC configurations, so the following year, we introduced online configuration. Customers visiting the site could select a system, add or subtract various combinations of components, such as memory, disk drives, video adapters, modems, network adapters, sound cards, speakers, and the like, and have the final price of their system calculated in real time. Back then, they still had to talk to a sales representative to complete the sale, but customers got an electronic taste of the advantages of the direct model.

I remember being surprised at how fast general knowledge of the Internet was spreading. We had a big meeting at 3M around that time, and the first thing their CIO said to me was, "I really like your website."

---

*That figure was later changed to $300 billion by the year 2002.

That blew me away. It was that kind of early feedback that gave me the confidence to say, "The Internet is going to be mainstream and we need to be all over it."

THE ULTIMATE EXTENSION OF DIRECT

It was the right time to expand the capabilities of *www.dell.com* to include online sales. I said so in a presentation to the Board of Directors, with the help of Scott Eckert, who was my executive assistant at the time and later went on to play a key role in developing our online business. The basic thesis: The Internet will fundamentally change the way that companies do business through its ability to enable people to conduct low-cost, one-to-one customer interactions with rich content. Specifically, I knew it could make a significant difference to Dell.

As I saw it, the Internet offered a logical extension of the direct model, creating even stronger relationships with our customers. The Internet would augment conventional telephone, fax, and face-to-face encounters, and give our customers the information they wanted faster, cheaper, and more efficiently.

In addition to researching, configuring, pricing, and ordering our products online, customers could use the Internet to check the status of their order as it moved down the manufacturing line. If they had questions about how it worked, they could go to our technical support page, where they would have access to all of the same information that our own technical support teams did. The Internet would make the direct model even more direct.

The benefits to Dell were equally compelling. The Internet applied to all of Dell's customer base, so it would serve as a useful tool to further identify and target different market segments. It would work not just within the United States but all over the world. It met our requirements for scaleable infrastructure: The one-to-one nature of Internet transactions meant that we could increase our sales volume without drastically increasing our company head count, because our salespeople could devote more time to higher-value activities rather than to mundane tasks.

By improving the speed and flow of information, the Internet would lower costs for us, and consequently, for our customers. Ultimately, Dell is a company with lots of transactions: order status, configurations, price. Each of those transactions costs money. On the Internet, there is almost no cost whatsoever for those transactions. Right now we have more than 2 million people visiting our website every week. But it wouldn't matter whether that number was .2 million or 20 million—the cost difference would be trivial. With each additional transaction on *www.dell.com*, we would be saving our customers money by lowering our overhead. This would create even more value for our customers while enhancing our competitive advantage.

In June 1996, we began selling desktops and notebooks over the Internet. We added servers later that year.

ACHIEVING LIFTOFF

In doing our own market research, we quickly discovered that corporate accounts, our biggest market, were initially more hesitant than individual consumers about the idea of buying computers over the Internet. Consumer e-mail was telling us that after configuring their machines and generating a price quote, visitors were eager to click a mouse and make a purchase. So we decided to focus on consumers first and use this experience to build a better understanding of how we might best approach the corporate market, which is by far the largest portion of our business.

But we didn't do any advance advertising. Before we announced to the world that we were selling online, we wanted to be sure we could execute, and execute well. So we quietly launched the site, and before we knew it, we were getting tens of thousands of visitors—especially tech-savvy customers. And when we decided to start mentioning our website in our regular advertising, we tapped into another huge pool of knowledgeable customers who hadn't yet realized that they could buy from us online. By December 1996, we were generating sales of approximately $1 million a day.

That figure made everyone sit up and take notice. At the time, Amazon.com was doing $15 million worth of business a quarter selling books online and operating at a loss. When we came out and said that we were doing $1 million a day *and* making money, the industry spotlight turned on us. The attention achieved exactly what we wanted. It drove traffic to *www.dell.com* and helped us establish a leadership position.

Assuming a leadership position in Internet commerce had been one of our objectives. We wanted to define the Internet business model so that it became an extension of our direct model rather than just an adjunct to some complex reseller relationship. For example, if you went to our competitors' sites to buy a computer, you'd be given one of two options: an 800 number to call for the location of the nearest dealer or, if you entered your address, directions to the nearest dealer. Meanwhile, our customers were logging onto *www.dell.com*, configuring the system that best suited their needs, entering their credit card number, and making a purchase right then and there.

We already knew the direct model gave us a fundamental advantage; we realized how great that advantage could be through the Internet. *www.dell.com* was a lightning rod both for attention to the company and to the direct business model, equating the company with Internet commerce. And today, every time you see Dell mentioned in the context of e-commerce, you see *www.dell.com*. It's a self-perpetuating momentum generator. The more people see it, the more go to the site, and the more likely they are to buy something online.

This is the value of being out in front with the best version of a good idea, instead of being the twenty-eighth guy to show up with a website—no matter how good it is.

WAGING A CAMPAIGN OF INTERNAL EVANGELISM

One of the sayings around Dell is that if you want to get people to think big, you need to act big. We were certainly thinking big when we set about constructing a successful Internet model. We didn't want to just set up an online store as an appendage to our business. A lot of businesses who look at the Internet simply as a way to launch electronic sales are missing the point. The real potential of the Internet is its ability to speed information flow, and that affects all kinds of transactions.

We wanted the Internet to become a key part of our entire business system. We wanted to make the Internet the first point of contact for every customer and prospect, and we planned for 50 percent of all customer transactions to be online within a few years.

To execute these objectives, we had to act big. We provided enthusiastic executive sponsorship of the initiative to integrate the Internet into every part of our business model. Rather than just using the Internet in our sales and configuration systems, we decided to employ Internet technology throughout all of our information systems, in order to connect more quickly and efficiently with customers and suppliers. Our information technology perspective was—and still is—to reduce obstacles to the origin and flow of information, and to simplify the systems in an effort to really maximize our business processes.

I had said, "Look, anything that we produce, whether it's a business card or a box or a piece of direct mail or a letter or a ROM-BIOS, anything that has our name on it should have *www.dell.com* on it." There was no part of the company that was exempt. I'd rather overkill a great idea than underexploit it.

Thanks to an intense marketing campaign, *www.dell.com* was

showing up everywhere: in advertisements, on company business cards, on every box coming out of the factory, even on a sign pointing to the men's rest room at a European management team meeting in Germany.

Inside the company, however, there were people who didn't understand how the Internet would change our business. To make sure everyone in the company was Internet-literate, we conducted a campaign of internal evangelism. We went into the cubes and high traffic points and plastered them with posters showing me in an Uncle Sam pose with the caption, "Michael wants YOU to know the Net!" I sent out a company-wide e-mail describing Dell's Internet strategy and how easy it is to place an order through *www.dell.com*, then asked all our managers to buy a book through Amazon.com so that they could familiarize themselves with Internet commerce. We sponsored a scavenger hunt for people to find information on the Web. We set up an online literacy quiz called "Know The Net" and challenged all our people to take it. We also gave every employee throughout the company globally access to the Internet and our own Intranet and encouraged their use.

A surprising percentage of our people also weren't aware of how the Internet could help our business. Sales and service departments didn't understand its implications and were fearful, at first, that the Net would automate their jobs away. We invested a lot in educating our sales representatives, especially the field-based account executives who own customer relationships. We showed them how the Internet made them more effective while also providing a value-added service for the customer. The reps soon saw that *www.dell.com* was a source of highly qualified leads. They could close sales with fewer calls and have greater reach within existing accounts. With our growth rates, there was more than enough business for everybody.

Some might argue that if you give employees access to the World Wide Web, they will spend all their time surfing the Net. But that's like saying, "We don't want to teach our people how to read because they might spend all their time reading." That's the wrong way to approach it. As a resource, the Internet enables and enhances so many business functions—if you're preoccupied with the ways in which your staff might abuse the technology, you're going to miss out on the benefits while your competitors run away with the future.

I remember talking with one of our customers about this. They actually did a measurement to see how much nonbusiness time their employees spent on the Internet. It came out to six minutes a day. That's less time than most people spend on one personal phone call. My feeling is, if you're an employee at Dell and you occasionally go online to order a book, you're saving thirty minutes that you otherwise would have spent going to the bookstore!

For us, the issue wasn't whether people would waste time on the Internet but whether they would use the Internet enough. Not to become completely familiar with a transformative business tool like the Internet is just foolish—especially when it's an integral part of your company's strategy and competitive advantage.

We faced a similar crossroads years ago, around 1986, when we first started using e-mail. People would ask me, "How do you get your employees to use e-mail?" My response was, "That's easy. You just ask them if they got that note you sent them on e-mail." No one likes to be uninformed, right?

One of the things that makes the Internet so exciting is that it brings the outside in. In today's marketplace, you can't afford to become insulated in your own activities. Our industry changes so quickly that if we don't constantly refresh our knowledge and stay in front of new technologies and concepts, we'll quickly become obsolete. The Internet allows us to bring in an outside point of view, whether it's a customer perspective or news about our competitors or developments in other areas of the world.

Before I visit a customer, I always log on to their website to see how much I can learn about their company. I can get a real flavor of the company and its culture from its website. Certainly I'll be more fluent as a result of looking at their website than I would be from reading a static annual report with a bunch of pretty pictures. We want everyone in our company to be doing that, so that we better understand our customers, our competitors, our suppliers, our market, and the world around us.

CONVERTING BIG BUSINESS

As I've mentioned, our early Internet business was primarily consumer- and small business-oriented because for many of those customers, purchasing online was a natural next step after getting product information and price quotes online. Convincing corporate accounts to buy online, however, was much more difficult. They felt we were asking them to radically change the way they purchased. Many of our large customers have deeply ingrained purchasing systems, and they didn't know how they could exchange information between those systems and the Internet. Some were concerned about the security of their information online. And for still others, the act of deciding what to buy and the decision to actually buy it are two different events, often handled by at least two different people or departments. We solved that problem by creating a purchasing process that allowed the two events to be handled separately.

Driving change in your own organization is hard enough; driving change in other organizations is nearly impossible. But I believed—and still believe—that the Internet would become as pervasive and invaluable as the telephone. We knew it was too important to our business—and potentially, to our customers' businesses—to wait for them to figure it out for themselves. So we assumed the responsibility of educating our customers on the basic benefits of doing things electronically.

Our account reps were our educating mechanism. They asked

customers, "How are you doing business with Dell today?" The message we needed to get across was that ordering online simplifies things: There's less chance for error in making an order and a better means of tracking it. Ordering online is more efficient because it funnels the same information though one route rather than three.

That one route is a customized page on our website called "Dell Premier Pages." When we started setting up Premier Pages, we initially thought, "Gee, this is a great way to provide e-commerce for our customers." But it would later turn out that although a lot of companies wanted the simplicity of doing business with us online, what they especially appreciated were the value-added services our Internet connection ultimately could provide.

Each company's Premier Page gives its employees Internet access to password-protected, customer-specific information about Dell's products and services. Customers can configure, price, and buy systems at the agreed-on price. They can track orders and inventory through detailed account purchasing reports by group, geographic location, product, average unit price, and total dollar value, so that they can better manage their assets. They can access contact information for Dell account, service, and support team members. They can check an order and find out if their system is sitting on the FedEx dock in Memphis, and how soon they can expect delivery. If a customer wants to find out how many PCs the company ordered for its European operations, he can access our data warehouse, type in the parameters, and dynamically generate reports.

We've also increased the scope of our online asset management, so that we can let customers know whether their systems are Year 2000 compliant, when their lease is due to run out, or when it's time to upgrade to a new computer.

Premier Pages are not a substitute for a live sales representative. Instead, they augment the sales rep's functions. The relationship is similar to that between a customer and a bank. For major transactions, customers want to talk directly to a real person; other times, they're happy to use an ATM.

MOVING INFORMATION IN REAL-TIME

I was online one night when I received a note from one of the people in our server group. He had built an addition to our Intranet site, focused on servers. There was a section on our global alliances with Microsoft, Intel, Oracle, and other partners; a demonstration of all the advertisements we've run with them; a list of all our joint announcements; and a catalog of all our products and tools. The server site basically gave our sales teams a robust series of tools that they can access wherever they are, to help them conduct their business. It's very clearly organized, always updated, and because it's online, always available.

To do the same thing in the physical world, you would need a loose-leaf binder so huge that most people couldn't even lift it. Trying to update a physical system like that would be a nightmare, involving tens of thousands of people. But online, it's one of those magical tasks that can be accomplished almost instantaneously. The end result is a richer, more efficient, more accessible information system. And it's global, too.

The Internet—and the company's internal Intranet—let us shrink the amount of time it takes for the organization to get up to speed on a new topic or to share best practices across the company. It eliminates the physical forms of information that take more time and cost more money to deliver.

We used to attach files to e-mail documents when we wanted people to review information. Then one day, I was in a meeting and said, "Gee, wouldn't it be great if we could review information over the Internet so that our network capacity wasn't strained by all of these charts and graphs flowing back and forth."

Today, we put an Internet or Intranet address in the e-mail, so that people can click on the hyperlink to access the information. We used to get performance reports once a week. Now we can go to the Net and get the information in real time.

It's impossible for any sales organization to understand the breadth and depth of all the products a company offers. But it's easy to describe and explain them on the Internet and to update them as frequently as necessary so that salespeople have a readily accessible reference guide. If we have a new product being introduced in the next few months, we can provide information to our sales and support teams immediately. We no longer have to sit around the proverbial campfire and tell one guy to pass it on to the next.

We can put complex white papers online that explain new technology and provide diagrams of how machines are configured. This way, users can get a great feel for what our products do — much better than they would get from a static brochure or some other noninteractive method of information. They can get as much detail as they desire. And we know that they've read it. If we send out a physical piece of mail to our customers, not only do we not know whether they've received or read it, we can't possibly know which pages they read or which they found especially helpful. But we can measure clicks in the online world, so we know exactly what information our customers find valuable.

The ability to measure customer response in a scientific way is just remarkable. We can do some of this in the physical world with dedicated toll-free numbers for specific advertisements that tell us which ads generate how many calls and how many of those calls translate into sales. But on the Internet you can do real-time experiments. You can present an offer to customers and within two hours you know whether that offer is successful. You can even change the offer slightly and compare the results of the different offers in real-time, then switch to whichever one seems to be the most effective — literally within minutes.

There's a tremendously rich feedback loop with the Internet. The adjustments and refinements that go into traditional marketing are based on the course corrections that might occur every month or every couple of months. On the Internet, course corrections happen much, much faster. Consequently, the cost of conducting an experiment has gone down considerably, and it costs almost nothing to make a correction.

HYPERLINK TO THE FUTURE

When we first began using the Internet to expand our business, we had three basic objectives: to make it easier to do business with Dell, to reduce the cost of doing business with Dell, and to enhance our customer relationships. Many said we couldn't make it on the Internet. Many of these were the same people who said that the direct business model would never work and that we could never sell servers direct.

As I write this, Dell is selling more than $35 million per day over the Internet. And the Internet has become part of the business mainstream. In 1996, there were 175 Fortune 500 companies with their own website. By the end of 1997, the number had more than doubled. By 1999, only two percent of the Fortune 500 compnaies did not have a website.

But for Dell, online commerce was only the beginning. Because we viewed the Internet as a central part of our IT strategy, we started to view the ownership of information differently, too. Rather than closely guarding our information databases, which took us years to develop, we used Internet browsers to essentially give that same information to our customers and suppliers—bringing them literally *inside* our business. This became the key to what I call a virtually integrated organization—an organization linked not by physical assets, but by information. By using the Internet to speed information flow between companies, essentially eliminating inter-company boundaries, it would be possible to achieve precision and speed-to-market for products and services in ways not dreamed possible before.

It would be the ultimate business system for a digital economy.

I can't say I knew how my early experimentation with electronic bulletin boards would come full circle, to selling billions of dollars' worth of systems over the Internet. Nor did I fully realize how far my adventures in selling computers out of my dorm room would take us. We certainly had our share of rough times, especially when the company was still young. But by following the courage of our convictions and keeping our eyes on what mattered most—our customers, our shareholders, and our people—Dell thrived.

Out of these experiences, our strategies for success were born: speed to market; superior customer service; and a fierce commitment to producing consistently high quality, custom-made computer systems that provide the highest performance and the latest relevant technology to our customers. And, as we as a company evolved, our strategies became more robust. I may have been fascinated with eliminating unnecessary steps, but once I bypassed the middleman and sold directly to customers, I set my sights on tightening the relationships we had with suppliers, reducing the number of steps involved in managing inventory, and improving the cost and time-to-market advantages we provided to our customers. Telephone sales worked just fine for a long time—and still do, for some customers—until we exploited the limitless potential of the Internet.

Part Two of this book is devoted to how we capitalized on the lessons learned in the first fifteen years of our company's history to become the second-largest manufacturer and marketer of personal computers in the world. In the next chapters, you will see how we forge powerful partnerships with our people, customers, and suppliers to achieve maximum results. Among other things, you'll learn how we maintain the high-energy culture of a start-up even though we're twenty-five thousand strong; who and how we hire; and why we actually reduce our managers' responsibilities as a reward for their success. You'll see why we design all of our products with our customers in mind—even when the competition doesn't; the various ways we get data from our customers, and how we've utilized that close relationship to gain a huge advantage over our competitors. You'll understand why, when dealing with any kind of supplier, certain precepts—like fewer is better, complacency kills, and proximity pays—are doctrine. And you'll see these precepts help us turn our inventory—and deliver our products to the end-user—faster than anyone else in our industry.

We'll even detail how Dell handles the competition, as well as what we expect for the future of the Internet in a truly connected economy.

No one company does everything right, always. That much we know. But we learned our lessons the hard way: through experience. Perhaps, from our example, you will learn something about developing and honing your competitive edge in business, too.

Part II

CREATE A
POWERFUL PARTNERSHIP

I **'M OFTEN ASKED HOW WE MANAGE TO** maintain the attitude of a challenger, even as we continue to grow at record speeds. Culture is, by far, one of the most enigmatic facets of management that I've encountered.

It is also one of the most important. Once a reporter asked me which of our competitors represented the biggest threat to Dell. I said the greatest threat to Dell wouldn't come from a competitor.

It would come from our people.

It hasn't been easy, trying to maintain the entrepreneurial spirit that has characterized Dell as our company has grown bigger (in terms of headcount) and more complicated (by way of infrastructure). Nor has it been easy to maintain the energy of a focused team, as we've expanded around the world. But my goal has always been to make sure that everyone at Dell feels they are a part of something great—something special—perhaps something even greater than themselves.

In this chapter are our strategies for finding and developing a great team that can deliver results. Then, in Chapter Nine, I'll go beyond the creation of a winning culture to show how leveraging talent can prove to be an invaluable competitive advantage.

Simply put, the best way I know to establish and maintain a healthy, competitive culture is to partner with your people—through shared objectives and a common strategy.

DEVELOP ONE TEAM, ONE STRATEGY

The ability to find and hire the right people can make or break your business. It is as plain as that. No matter where you are in the life cycle of your business, bringing in great talent should always be a top priority. It's also one of the hardest objectives to meet.

I remember looking at Dell's three-year plan back in 1994 and seeing our potential to grow between 40 percent and 50 percent a year. That meant that the company would more than double in size every two years. We were challenged running a $3 billion business. It was clear that to get to $7 billion or $10 billion we would need to hire and develop lots of additional talent.

At Dell, what ties us all together is belief in our direct model. In people terms, that translates into responsibility to one another, accountability for results, and an appreciation for facts and data. Over time, we have developed a laser-focused strategy that we take great pains to communicate consistently and thoroughly throughout the entire global organization. We have created established benchmarks for success, based on the achievement of the company's goals and tied directly to the value we create for our customers and shareholders. And we do our best to articulate our objectives clearly. People who thrive at Dell are results-oriented, self-reliant, and driven to lead. We give them the authority to drive the business in a particular direction, and provide them with the tools and resources they need to accomplish their goals.

Whether you're hiring someone in an entry-level position or to run one of your largest groups, that person must be completely in sync with the company's business philosophy and objectives. If the person thinks in a way that's compatible with your company values and beliefs, and understands what the company does and is driven to do, he will not only work hard to fulfill his immediate goals, but he will also contribute to the greater goals of the organization. Think about it: If one of our primary values at Dell is to provide a superior customer experience, and the service person answering the phone is curt or unfriendly, or leaves a caller on hold for too long, we're through. It doesn't matter how informed the sales rep would be, or how quickly the product would arrive, or how pleased that customer would be with her system. She's already hung up.

That's not to say we look for one "right" kind of person or personality, nor do we encourage "herd" thinking. We would die without the imagination and innovation of our people. But everyone is mobilized around a customer-oriented focus. That makes all the difference in the world.

In ways large and small, employees at every level can help to forward your company strategy and achieve goals beyond their immediate area of responsibility, but only if your company is genuinely devoted to their long-term growth and development. That's why you need to hire ahead of the game.

HIRE AHEAD OF THE GAME

It's not enough to hire to fill a job. It's not even enough to hire on the basis of one's talents. You have to hire based upon a candidate's potential to grow and develop.

I learned this lesson early in the company's history. I interviewed carefully and tried to hire just the right people to fill the jobs that were open. And yet even then, when we were much smaller, we were growing at a furious rate, and before I knew it, some who had been qualified suddenly were out of their league. I had hired them because they were good at what they did, not necessarily good for what they were going to have to do in the future. When a company is growing quickly, even talented people can become overwhelmed. You have to find people who can do one job well while simultaneously growing into a new one.

Today we hire people with the long-term in mind. We're not bringing them in to do a job; we're inviting them to join the company. If it's a great match, their jobs are likely to change many, many times as we segment the business, and as we focus more heavily on some areas rather than others. If you hire people with the potential to grow far beyond their current position, you build depth and additional capacity into your organization. That's critical when you face the next wave of growth or the next competitive challenge.

We recruit for succession. And, in fact, we institutionalize it. Everyone's job includes finding and developing their successor—not just when they are ready to move into a new role, but as an ongoing part of their performance plan.

What should you look for in today's candidates to ensure tomorrow's leadership? At Dell we look for people who possess the questioning nature of a student and are always ready to learn something new. Because so much of what has contributed to our success goes against the grain of conventional wisdom, we look for those who have an open, questioning mind: we look for people who have a healthy balance of experience and intellect; people who aren't afraid to make a mistake in the process of innovation; and people who expect change to be the norm and are liberated by the idea of looking at problems or situations from a different angle and coming up with unprecedented solutions.

And whenever humanly possible, I look for them myself.

OWN THE RECRUITMENT PROCESS

I'm always actively looking for good people, and I expect others on our team to do the same.

And I don't restrict my search to managers. Often, I'll meet with our summer interns, not to interview them per se, but to see what they're getting out of their experiences at Dell, hear what their observations are, and see what new perspectives they have on the company. If they've had a good experience at Dell, and their strengths match our objectives, many will join our company and go on to succeed.

When I interview people, the first thing I do is find out how they process information. Are they thinking in economic terms? What is their definition of success? How do they relate to people? Do they really understand the strategy of the business they're involved in today? Do they understand ours? It's surprising how many people already in the workforce contribute in some way to their company's strategy but don't really understand it that well. It's important to me to know whether potential candidates have the capacity to understand Dell's strategy and if they can help us evolve and develop it.

I usually ask candidates to tell me about something they did that they are particularly proud of. This gives me a few insights into whether they are focused on the success of the company they're currently working for or on their own personal aggrandizement. Then I will almost always make a point of actively disagreeing with them. I want to know if they have strong opinions and are willing to defend them. At Dell, we need people who are confident enough of their own abilities and strong in their convictions, not people who feel the need to agree in the face of conflict.

REWARD SUCCESS BY NARROWING RESPONSIBILITY

Any senior-level executive, manager, or small business owner would agree: The right people in the right jobs are instrumental to a company's success. Traditionally, when a talented employee masters a job, he gets promoted to a new job that has broader responsibilities, a larger staff, and a bigger budget. But what do you do when job responsibilities are increasing by half again every year, simply as a function of the company's growth?

If you assume that your people can grow at the same rate as your company—and still maintain the sharp focus that is critical to success—you will be sadly disappointed. When a business is growing quickly, many jobs grow laterally in responsibility, becoming too big and complex for even the most ambitious, hardest-working person to handle without sacrificing personal career development or becoming burned out.

It doesn't make sense to stay true to a structure that makes it more difficult for your people to succeed. Your organizational structure must be flexible enough to evolve along with your people, rather than work against them.

This is one of the biggest and most challenging cultural issues we face as a fast-growing company. Our solution is segmentation.

Originating with sales and growing into an overall organizing force, segmentation as a strategy drove the ways in which we reorganized the company for success. But as the company continued to grow, we began thinking that segmentation could also serve as a way to create jobs that gave our people renewed inspiration and opportunity for development, as well as the chance to focus more sharply on a narrower range of responsibilities. At Dell, increased focus almost always means more growth.

Segmenting a job happens a couple of ways. We'll bring in additional talent and/or divide a business unit, product organization, or functional unit in some way that makes the newly segmented structure more manageable and more sharply focused to the business opportunity. This allows us to keep our people happy and thriving and maintain a high growth rate.

When we first started doing this, some people were confused— and understandably so. Traditionally, narrowed responsibilities are a sign of demotion, disapproval, or failure. At other companies, people are evaluated by the size of their staff or how many dollars they generate. At Dell, success means growing so fast that we take half your business away. Even when we create two or sometimes three new groups out of one, the new group is often twice as big as the original one had been, say, two years ago.

One way we've found useful in overcoming employee concern is not only to plan the organizational structure for the future, but also to communicate this "future state" broadly within the organization. This allows constant incremental organizational adjustment. Organizational changes are completed *by* a given date, not done all at once *on* that date.

These early communications have proven to be motivational to employees because they're able to see in advance the tangible impact of growth on their job opportunities and careers.

Job segmentation is completely counterintuitive to conventional business practice. But the underlying logic makes perfect sense: We want good people to thrive and help us continue to prosper. It's the best way we know to create meaningful new jobs that more precisely match an employee's skill set. There is no added value in expecting people to be supermen or superwomen. In that case, you might as well expect them to fail.

Job segmentation also facilitates our corporate strategy by helping us identify our weaknesses. We may not realize that we're lacking in the finance or marketing areas of the company until we consider segmenting. Once we do, we may discover that we don't have enough people to assume the new responsibilities. As a check and balance system, it's very practical.

But the best thing about segmentation is that it allows us to create new opportunities for people. New businesses get started and holes in the organization emerge which encourage people to grow. Segmentation helps ensure that our best people don't become complacent or bored, and that our relationship will be a long and, we hope, fruitful one.

SEGMENT THE CEO

I have segmented my own job twice. Back in 1993–1994, it was becoming very clear to me that there was far too much to be done and far more opportunities than I could pursue myself. Not to take advantage of these opportunities because of a self-limiting notion would have been a great shame. That was one of the reasons I asked Mort Topfer to join the company.

Our partnership is a classic example of job segmentation: We've come to know that two heads are better than one. Mort and I have complementary strengths so we each focus on the areas where we feel we can contribute the most value. It's a divide and conquer approach, marked by constant communication and shared decision-making, which multiplies our individual capacities for success.

As the company continued to grow, we again segmented the job. In 1997, we promoted Kevin Rollins, who had been a key member of our executive team since 1996, to what we now call the office of the chairman. The three of us together run the company. We still find ourselves with more opportunities than we know what to do with, but the shared responsibility definitely frees us up to pursue those where we feel we can add the most value.

We don't all agree all the time. But we share a sense of accountability and responsibility and a set of common objectives. It's not a case of "I do my job and you do yours." We work together, within the same framework of a consistent strategy, unified goals, constant communication, and clear areas of focus.

ENFORCE TEAM-WIDE ACCOUNTABILITY

I've always been fascinated by how and why teams work—or don't work—together. But it's become especially important as Dell continues to grow and we hire so many new people. How do you keep the focus, the camaraderie, and the organizational intimacy of a small company when you get that big?

Again, you have to figure out ways to align and blend everyone's talents to create value for your customers and shareholders.

Aligning a team toward a common objective and creating the same incentive system across the entire company helps drive this point home with your people. On our factory floor, for example, people work in teams of two to receive, manufacture, and pack an order for delivery to a customer. Their profit-sharing incentive encourages them to be productive as a team. Hourly metrics (or data) are posted on monitors on the factory floor so that each team has a sense of how it is doing against our goals. The more efficient our manufacturing teams are, the more they stand to gain.

They know that it is more beneficial to work together rather than apart.

The principle behind the 360-degree performance appraisal is similar. Instead of gauging an employee's annual progress against the subjective views of one person—usually her direct supervisor—this full circle review solicits input from everyone an employee works with. It's a great measurement for identifying those areas that might require further development or improvement, and it keeps people focused on achieving their goals as a team. It's the closest we've come to objectifying the data on our people, minimizing interpersonal politics. As a result, we've seen stronger team members spend extra time and effort with others who seem to be having trouble keeping up because it's in their interest to do so. One of the ways they do that is by openly sharing the results of their 360 evaluations with one another. This allows our management teams to work together on individual areas for improvement.

This kind of teamwork suggests a different way of building a company together. It's not about people staying out of each other's way, or working hard to be competitive but not political. It's about people who are thoroughly invested in each other's growth.

It is, in the truest sense of the word, a partnership.

MAKE THE MOST OF INCIDENTAL INTERACTIONS

Dell is the kind of company where everyone rolls up his sleeves and gets personally involved. We may be a $30 billion company but our entire management team, myself included, is involved in the details of our business every day. This is, in fact, how we got to be successful: As managers, it's not enough to sit around theorizing and reviewing what those who report to us do. We frequently meet with customers and attend working-level meetings about products, procurement, and technology, to tap into the real source of our company's experience and brainpower.

Why bother? It's a way to get close to our people, for certain. But that's not all. Our day-to-day involvement in the business helps us establish and allows us to maintain one of Dell's critical competitive advantages: speed. In this case, "staying involved in the details" allows for rapid decision making because we know what's going on.

For example, when a problem crops up, there's no need for us to do more research or assign someone the job of figuring out what the issues are. Because we often have all the information at our fingertips, we can gather the right people in one room, make a decision, and move forward—fast. The pace of business moves too quickly these days to waste time noodling over a decision. And while we strive to always make the right choice, I believe it's better to be first at the risk of being wrong than it is to be 100 percent perfect two years too late.

You can't possibly make the quickest or best decisions without data. Information is the key to any competitive advantage. But data doesn't just drop by your office to pay you a visit. You've got to go out and gather it.

I do this by roaming around.

I don't want my interactions planned; I want anecdotal feedback. I want to hear spontaneous remarks. I want to come upon someone who's teaching an elderly woman how to turn her system on for the first time. I want to happen upon someone who is stumped by a customer's question—and help answer it if I can. I want to experience this, because this is what our employees' days are made of, and it arms me with relevant information to make the best decisions on behalf of our customers and our people.

Some days I show up at our headquarters building; other days, I'll go to some of our other facilities. I show up at the factory unannounced to talk to the people on the floor and to see what's really going on. I go to brown-bag lunches two or three times a month, and meet with a cross-section of people from all across the company. It's easy to sit in a product meeting and say, "We have these new products and our salespeople will sell them." But this may not be the reality. So I go to a brown-bag lunch and listen carefully to what the sales force has to say. It's a great way of learning what people are really dealing with on a day-to-day basis, and provides a forum for the exchange of ideas and solutions.

I believe you can learn a lot from incidental interactions. I might be in a car with an account executive as we drive from one customer to another. That's a great opportunity to find out what's really going on. I'll ask, "What are your customers telling you? How do you think the company's products are doing? What are you seeing in the competitive market? What are our biggest challenges? What are the threats to your success? How can the company support you better?" The qualitative data are as important as the quantitative data in terms of keeping our people motivated and our focus on target.

I also enjoy roaming around outside the company to see what people think of us. On the Web, nobody knows I'm a CEO. I'll hang out in chatrooms where actual users commonly chat about Dell and our competitors. I listen to their conversations as they discuss their purchases and their likes and dislikes. It's a tremendous learning opportunity.

One of my goals is to continually bring information from the outside world into Dell, with an eye toward staying as competitive as we can. As your company grows ever larger and your job becomes more complex, you run the risk of spending most of your time talking to yourself. That's a dangerous thing to do. We must constantly immerse ourselves in what our customers are saying, what our markets are saying, and what's going on in the world around us in order to stay competitive.

I wish it were possible for me to interact with everyone at Dell as I used to. But it's not possible to scale the number of interactions to be consistent with the growth of the company. When a company grows from 1,000 employees to 25,000 employees, simple mathematics dictate that I'm twenty-five times less likely to see any individual employee.

But that doesn't mean I care twenty-five times less. To the contrary, I miss the close connection that we had when we were all cramped together in our first real office space. We've found there are, however, things you can do to bridge the distance between you and your people in a larger organization, and develop the fast-paced, flexible culture that's a source of competitive advantage:

◆ Mobilize your people around a common goal. Help them to feel a part of something genuine, special, and important, and you'll inspire real passion and loyalty.

◆ Invest in mutual long-term goals by hiring ahead of the game and communicating this commitment to your people.

◆ Don't leave the talent search to the human resources folks—or get caught up in hiring "inside the box." In today's economy, talent is in short supply.

◆ Cultivate a commitment to personal growth. Success isn't static—and your culture shouldn't be, either. Pay attention to what your best people are achieving, and build an infrastructure that rewards mastery. The best way to keep the most talented people is to allow their jobs to change with them. Sometimes, reducing their responsibilities will give them the space to tackle new opportunities and to expand—and your business will expand, too.

◆ Get involved. Even if you can't go on sales calls, or drop by meetings, use e-mail or the Internet to stay in touch with people at all levels of the organization and especially with those in faraway locations whom you don't see as often as you'd like. Think of this as a way of immersing yourself in real information, with real people, that will allow you to react in real time.

Connecting with the outside world keeps you aware. Connecting with your people—your most valuable asset—is the way to keep your business and your people healthy and strong.

Elevating that talent to a competitive advantage is the next step.

BUILD A COMPANY
OF OWNERS

IT'S ONE THING TO CREATE A CULTURE that works. It's another to use that culture to create a measurable strategic advantage.

At Dell, much of our success can be attributed to our people. But it's not enough to just hire well. You need to engender a sense of personal investment in all your employees—which comes down to three things: responsibility, accountability, and shared success.

As a manager, you know that individual "investment" is almost impossible to inspire externally—some people have it, and some people don't. It's a quality that is usually self-motivated.

Unless you can develop a company of owners.

Creating a culture in which every person in your organization, at every level, thinks and acts like an owner means that you need to aim to connect individual performance with your company's most important objectives. For us, that means we mobilize everyone around creating the best possible customer experience and enhancing shareholder value—and we use specific quantitative measurements of our progress toward those goals that apply to every employee's performance. A company composed of individual owners is less focused on hierarchy and who has the nicest office, and more intent on achieving their goals.

At Dell, everyone's an owner. Here's how and why.

LEARN VORACIOUSLY

Our people are obviously motivated by the ways we link our goals to their compensation and incentives. But more importantly, there are ways in which we work to instill ownership thinking in our people and better leverage their talents so they can reach their full potential.

The willingness and ability to learn constantly is one of them. Let's face it: If we took all the knowledge we had gleaned from 1993 and 1994 and said, "That's all we need to know," I probably wouldn't be writing this book. But since the start of our company, we have had to learn at a voracious pace just to keep up. That's no small feat, given how quickly our jobs change.

I approach learning from the standpoint of asking questions: What would make your job at Dell easier? More successful? More meaningful? What do our customers like and not like? What do they need? What would they like to see us doing better? How can we improve? I start by asking a lot of questions and doing a lot of listening: You don't learn anything when you're talking. We spend a considerable amount of time opening the floor to questions at meetings, whether they're operations reviews or business updates or team meetings. We question the very issues at hand: Why are we doing this? Why aren't we doing that? Curiosity is encouraged because there's no operator's manual that contains all the answers. (And even if there were, we wouldn't want people to rely on it.)

I recently had a meeting with our Dell team in France. Someone asked, "Why is the company so focused on servers?" I answered by explaining how the profit pool works. "Think about it as a big pool of dollars that sits in the middle of the room. Every time we run in, we get to take some of that profit pool and run out. If we sell $1,000 PCs, we can run in as many times as we want but we don't get to take much out. But if we sell $10,000 servers, we can take a big handful of dollars. So, if all of you could run into the profit pool as many times as you wanted, what would you do—go after the $1,000 PC or the $10,000 server?"

This enabled them to relate to the concept of profit pools on a very immediate and personal level. The relevance of that example helped them "own" our server initiative and recognize that our ability to thrive depended on their ability to understand and sell servers to our customers.

The point is to get into the guts of why things happen. Asking lots of questions opens new doors to new ideas, which ultimately contributes to your competitive edge. In our procurement group, for example, someone responsible for buying disk drives knows to ask the deeper questions: What is the real cost structure that underlies the disk drive industry? If I were a disk drive manufacturer, what would my cost of capital be? What are the costs of the product components? What's my P&L? Who are my competitors? How will product ramps and technology evolution affect the cost structures? What are the economics of acquiring a customer like Dell over time? What are my incentives, and how will those motivate me to succeed? By understanding more fully the underlying economics from the standpoint of capital, supply chain, technology, and market trends, our people can make a much more informed series of decisions about the relationships we enter into.

We also learn a lot by asking the same questions in similar groups

across the company and comparing the results. We do this to share the
best ideas throughout our various businesses because we're all working
on the same team, toward the same goal. If one team is having great
success with medium-size companies, we cross-pollinate their ideas
around the world. If another team has figured out how to sell into law
firms, we share their learning throughout the organization. Our best
ideas can come from anywhere in the world and be shared instantly.
They help us develop the broad-reaching mindset required of a global
company. We exchange ideas through e-mail and the Web, and
through councils where we bring different groups from around the
world together to exchange information.

People have a tremendous capacity to grow and learn when stim-
ulated by this thought process. If we don't understand the significance of some new process or some new technology that is driving
our industry, if we don't understand the physics behind it and how it
will affect other suppliers, we run the risk of missing important technology transitions. As a result, we won't be equipped to make the right
decisions. But if we go back and understand the root cause of why
these things happen, we can make the right decisions and repeat the
process in the future.

That's how you obtain truly innovative thinking.

TEACH INNOVATIVE THINKING

It is really dangerous if everyone in a company starts thinking the
same way. And it can happen so easily, with everyone focused on the
same goals. The danger comes when you fall into the trap of
approaching problems too similarly.

You can encourage your people to think about your business, your
industry, your customers innovatively. Ask a different question—or
word the same question in a different way. By approaching a problem,
a response, or an opportunity from a different perspective, you create

an opportunity for new understanding and new learning. By questioning all the aspects of our business, we continually inject improvement and innovation into our culture.

How can we teach people to be more innovative? Ask them to approach a problem in a holistic sense. We start by asking our customers, "What would you really want this thing to do? Is there a different way to accomplish that?" We meet with our suppliers and ask, "Can we do this in a different way?" Then we try to come up with a totally different approach that exceeds the original objectives.

We did this in the mid–1990s when we introduced Managed PCs. At that time, the industry and media were all excited about what was presented as a brand-new product: the Network Computer, or NC. This supposedly revolutionary idea was essentially a stripped-down computer without a hard disk or floppy drive. All the software applications would reside on a large server, and the NC would only allow the user to run applications and access data at the center of the network.

The NC was announced with great hype at Comdex in November 1997. Soon, many were predicting it would ultimately spell the end of the PC as we know it, and several large computer companies were jumping on the bandwagon to develop and introduce their own versions of NCs.

The reality is, this was not a new idea at all. It was essentially an updated version of the "dumb terminal" of the 1980s, which had a small role in the computing spectrum and was massively overshadowed by the growth of PC usage. I doubted the NC would find much greater acceptance (but we still paid attention to it because it could have posed a potential threat to our business). Most users had come to rely too intensely on their PCs as a productivity tool: To remove all the flexibility and control over installed software would be almost as bad as taking away their PC and giving them a typewriter. In addition, mobile computing was becoming more important, and without a connection to the server, as on an airplane, an NC was totally useless.

But customer demand for NCs was beginning to build, so I challenged our product team to understand why. What was the underlying issue the NC was trying to solve, and what would be a better solution? If we didn't address it, we would certainly leave ourselves vulnerable.

It turned out that the NC provided the solution to a critical need experienced by many corporations. They needed to know how to maintain control over network standards and reduce the time and cost related to supporting users whose systems had crashed. In a way, the PC had become too flexible.

Our answer was Managed PCs. These are PCs that have the features, flexibility, and power that users had come to value, with remote management capabilities that allow network administrators to configure, manage, and maintain hardware and software from a central location.

Today, the NC is pretty much roadkill on the information superhighway. But nearly every company has developed some form of Managed PCs.

Our culture despises the status quo. We try to precondition our people to look for breakthrough ideas, so that when we're confronted with big strategic challenges, they can rise to the occasion and come up with the best solutions—fast. You must train your people to ask, on a regular basis, "How can we change the rules of the game? What can we do that no one ever thought of that enables us to achieve this goal?"

When you take the historical blinders off, it's amazing what you can accomplish. Having a history of successes based on unconventional wisdom encourages people to go for it. Fostering an environment that urges people to think like owners, in which they continually create new and different ideas, gives them the freedom and courage to take risks.

ENCOURAGE SMART EXPERIMENTATION

To encourage people to innovate more, you have to make it safe for them to fail. Many companies say that they welcome and expect innovation but also tell people, "Just don't screw up." Failure, however, takes on many different definitions.

If a team experiments with something and says, "These are the facts. This didn't work and here's why," that's not failure. That's a learning experience and, typically, an important milestone on the road to achieving success.

Our business is by definition full of innovation and experimentation because so many things that we try haven't ever been done before. We're facing new challenges and can't look to history because it's not relevant. Our website is a great example. When we started to sell computers over *www.dell.com*, we had to create an operational model from the ground up. That involved assembling a team of people from various groups within the company, and organizing them around one simple question: How do we accomplish this—and fast?

We're often faced with problems that we know represent an opportunity and it's up to us to create an entire business out of it. That's the fun stuff. But we also know that if we don't do it, someone else will. We're forced to innovate to stay ahead of the competition. And when you're dealing in an industry that's changing so dynamically, there are often more unknowns than knowns.

You also need to embrace an experimental attitude in making decisions. Sometimes you can't wait for all the data to present themselves before making a decision. You have to make the best decision you possibly can based on your experience, intuition, available data, and assessment of risk. There's a guaranteed element of risk in any business, so experiment—but experiment wisely.

Back in 1987, we expanded into the United Kingdom. It was a pretty big risk for a company that had only operated in the United

States, but once we succeeded there, it wasn't as big a deal to move into Canada and Germany. And once we knew that the direct model worked in those countries, it was logical to extend that to Sweden, France, and Japan. If you're smart about experimenting, it can lead to strategies that create new avenues of growth and ultimately become "business as usual."

We have deliberately shaped our culture to accept continual "course corrections" on the learning curve because in order to thrive, we need an environment in which people feel it's okay to experiment. Because we believe that people can learn from mistakes, we want them to feel good about trying something that's a little out of the ordinary with the goal of achieving something wonderful. It should be your goal to encourage experimentation in your people and, as a company, to experiment smarter than you ever have before.

BEWARE THE PERILS OF PRIDE

If you accept the status quo as "good enough," you're managing in a rearview mirror. And in this economy, you can bet you will end up smashing right into the future. Just to stay competitive, you have to constantly question everything you do.

Challenging the current state of affairs ensures that you don't get too wrapped up in your success. By now, self-criticism is ingrained in the Dell culture—we're always ready to question our own ideas, looking for ways things can be improved. We try to model this behavior from the top down. We hire for, and develop, leaders who are open-minded and can accept being disagreed with publicly or corrected when they've got their facts wrong. This helps promote open debate and encourages an intellectual meritocracy.

We try to avoid being too proud of our accomplishments. Some could argue that in certain areas, we've already set the benchmark. I'd like to think there are always ways to improve what we do. If we start to think we've made it, we're just setting ourselve up to be eclipsed by someone else.

It's not that pride in and of itself is a bad thing—it's wonderful to be proud of what you do every day and the company you do it for. Our people put a great deal of energy into the things that ultimately become the big accomplishments in our business; acknowledging their achievements reinforces the value that they bring to our company and emphasizes how much we appreciate their efforts.

But when taken too far, pride can create a false sense of security. Feeling invincible, people can assume that success begets success with little new effort—or even worse, that success happens all by itself. They can become blind to important trends or opportunities that are literally right in front of them. They can stop trying to find ever better new ways of doing things and may become oblivious to emerging threats. You would think that being featured on the cover of *Fortune* was a great achievement, but I'm quick to remind our team that in 1986 *Fortune* put a big, smiling picture of Digital Equipment's CEO, Ken Olsen, on the cover with the caption, "America's most successful entrepreneur: Ken Olsen." Since then, Digital's stock fell from about $200 a share to $20, then increased to $56 a share before they were acquired by Compaq—in part because the company never successfully made the move from a centralized proprietary computing model to a model based on industry standards.

Being on the cover of *Fortune* doesn't guarantee you anything.

It's easy to fall in love with how far you've come and how much you've done. It's definitely harder to see the cracks in a structure you've built yourself, but that's all the more reason to look hard and look often. Even if something seems to be working, it can always be improved.

DON'T TRY TO PERFUME A PIG

During the tough period of 1993 and 1994, one of the things I was most pleased with was the way we identified our problems head-on, without denying them or making excuses. We've tried to take the straightforward approach to mistakes and say, "We have a problem and we have to fix it." We know if we don't, someone else will.

It's hard to do that, though. It's human nature to shrink in the face of bad news or disappointment, and to hope that something will just happen to make the situation better. But something magical usually doesn't happen, and the time we waste in denial is always crucial. Things move so quickly that you need to be able to size up, almost instantaneously, what the problem is and start fixing it right away.

In a business based on a direct model, you get the facts immediately, whether you like them or not. We receive constant information on everything from our products to demand trends to quality data both in field performance and in our factories. Metrics are posted in the factories and throughout our company. Salespeople can measure their progress literally minute by minute. Almost every activity within the company has metrics attached to it, even so-called soft activities, such as legal, public relations, and human resources.

The metrics are more than figures and statistics; they also encompass customer feedback, whether it's great, bad, or downright ugly. We see the chance to talk with a customer who is not completely satisfied as an opportunity for self-improvement and learning, which helps us to hone our competitive edge.

One of our sayings is "Don't perfume the pig." By that we mean "Don't try to make something appear better than it really is." Sooner or later the truth will come out, and you are better off dealing with it head on.

When we're confronted with a business that's not performing well, we ask, "What's wrong here? Is this a business that ought to be performing well? Do we have a problem in execution, in strategy, or in management? Is it a business that will never work? Should we cut our losses now?"

You need to recognize the facts for what they are, rather than what you'd sometimes like them to be. If you have a clear set of expectations and metrics that are well understood by everyone, the issues tend to surface pretty quickly. Facing a problem and quickly accepting it enables you to address the issues immediately and move on problems faster.

Our people know they're either part of the problem or part of the solution. Our culture encourages a manager to stand up and say, "We've got a problem and we're not sure why it's happening." People need to know they can ask for help, especially when they're dealing with big, multidimensional problems.

The sooner the problems are identified, the sooner you can start to solve them.

COMMUNICATE, FAST AND DEEP

Almost anyone at Dell can explain the fundamental concepts that our business is based on. That's because we spend a tremendous amount of time communicating what's going on, what we're planning to do, and what everyone needs to do to help us achieve our goals. We do this in a number of different ways.

Every year, we have town hall meetings at which I describe how the company is doing, what our strategies are, where we stand in the market, and what our plans are. Then I answer lots of questions. Any question is okay. I keep my answers relatively simple and don't present them in corporate-speak. It's such a great opportunity to reiterate the objectives and mission of the company that we post a transcript on our Intranet for anyone who has to miss the meeting.

We celebrate successes both in person and electronically. We send out mass e-mail messages congratulating our teams on big wins, elevating their win to a company-wide accomplishment. It's exciting for people to hear about what's going on in different businesses or teams, and it also helps to share best practices, because one group benefits from what's working for others. It also helps build confidence throughout the organization.

When we started selling servers, for example, some of our salespeople weren't immediately comfortable with the idea. They were somewhat intimidated by the complexity of the technology and the expertise they needed to develop to succeed. So we started a standard feature in our weekly worldwide electronic newsletter called "Server Success." It depicted stories—from around the globe—of salespeople who had achieved big server wins: what obstacles they had to overcome, who the competition was, and what techniques they used to win. These electronic high-fives showed that success was indeed achievable.

Dell is not the kind of company in which messages languish. We have to "talk" in real-time through meetings, over e-mail, and on the Intranet because we're in a real-time business. Things happen in the morning that you have to react to by the afternoon. We have to be competitive twenty-four hours a day, 365 days a year, or else we lose business. A sense of urgency about communicating and solving problems is imperative.

All these strategies help to foster teamwork and individual accountability, both of which are key to maintaining an entrepreneurial edge. As one of my colleagues likes to say, "We're a bunch of entrepreneurs who work as a team."

STAY ALLERGIC TO HIERARCHY

We work hard to ensure that the direct relationships that characterize our business model also characterize our corporate structure. We have an open culture in which people feel comfortable taking the most direct route to get the information they need. E-mail is exchanged across traditionally "hierarchical" lines—this happens across all levels of the organization. We actively discourage anyone who thinks that just because he is a vice president, he should talk only to other vice presidents. An overly rigid hierarchical structure restricts information flow, which can't be good for anyone.

The same can be said for overly rigid business processes. In many organizations, management processes become etched in stone and create a permanent bureaucracy. At Dell, we realize processes serve the business—and not the other way around. We tell our people that if they can come up with a better process or solution for improving our business—and all the parties concerned agree—then they're free to change it.

In fact, I believe that much of the confusion that occurs in corporations today stems from stymied communication and complex hierarchies. We're allergic to hierarchy. Hierarchical structure to me fundamentally implies a loss of speed. It implies that there's congestion in the flow of information. It implies the need for layers of approval and command and control, and signoffs here, there, and everywhere. That's inconsistent with the speed with which we all need to make decisions, both as leaders and as a company, in this fast-paced marketplace.

Information in its raw form doesn't present itself in neat and tidy packages. That's why you must encourage the free flow of information at all levels. If something is worrying me, I'll cut to the chase and ask whoever it is who happens to know about it. Conversely, if an employee has a question, he knows he is encouraged to ask it, either through e-mail or at one of our meetings.

The point, of course, is not to circumvent management. Rather, the direct link often helps facilitate a greater knowledge and understanding of what's actually happening in the business and does so at a much greater speed. If an engineer in one of our product groups has an opinion about something, and it just so happens that customer input confirms his suspicion, I want to know. Random bits of information from sources both inside and outside the company won't always lead you to the answer, but they will assist you in focusing in on an emerging problem or opportunity or new idea.

MOBILIZE YOUR PEOPLE AROUND A SINGLE GOAL

Dell's culture reduces politics by focusing on results and aligning the interests of our employees with those of our shareholders. In addition to knowing their goals, you want the people in your company to have a real stake in its success.

At Dell, the vast majority of our employees are owners as well, a result of employee stock purchase plans, stock option grants, and a 401(k) plan in which we match employee contributions not with cash but with company stock. Stock ownership in the computer systems business is nothing new. At Dell, though, it comes with another commitment. To be an owner, you have to think like one. The personal investment people feel when they think and act like owners manifests itself in a true commitment to the company. I am surprised that most companies offering stock to their employees have missed this critical point.

To motivate an employee to think like an owner, you have to give her metrics she can embrace. At Dell, every employee's incentives and compensation are tied to the health of the business. And one of the best ways we've learned to evaluate its health is Return on Invested Capital, or ROIC. ROIC is a measure of how effectively Dell creates shareholder value relative to its cost of capital. In this way, ROIC helps allow you to identify your best-performing businesses and those that aren't delivering the performance they should.

We became interested in ROIC as a result of our experiences back in 1993. We had to sort through a variety of different businesses—selling through retail, selling to large companies, selling to small companies, selling to consumers, selling different types of products, selling in many different geographics, each with different characteristics—and figure out which ones were succeeding and which weren't. We determined successful strategies by measuring our return on invested capital and growth for each business. Where we were doing our jobs well, our businesses were delivering a high return on capital and a high level of growth.

ROIC became a focusing device. We introduced it in 1995 with a company-wide push to educate everyone about the benefits of a positive ROIC, with articles in the company newsletter, posters, talks by managers, and "Messages from Michael" devoted to the topic.

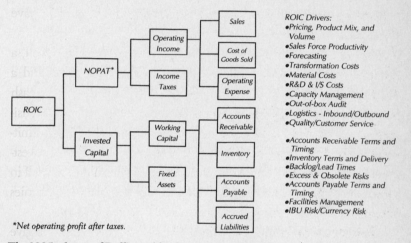

*Net operating profit after taxes.

ROIC Drivers:
- Pricing, Product Mix, and Volume
- Sales Force Productivity
- Forecasting
- Transformation Costs
- Material Costs
- R&D & I/S Costs
- Capacity Management
- Out-of-box Audit
- Logistics - Inbound/Outbound
- Quality/Customer Service

- Accounts Receivable Terms and Timing
- Inventory Terms and Delivery
- Backlog/Lead Times
- Excess & Obsolete Risks
- Accounts Payable Terms and Timing
- Facilities Management
- IBU Risk/Currency Risk

The 1995 edition of Dell's worldwide employee newspaper carried this chart showing the factors that lead to a return-on-invested-capital calculation.

We explained specifically how everyone could contribute: by reducing cycle times, eliminating scrap and waste, selling more, forecasting accurately, scaling operating expenses, increasing inventory turns, collecting accounts receivables efficiently, and doing things right the first time. And we make it the core of our incentive compensation program for all employees. We decided to reward employees around a matrix of ROIC and growth; higher performance directly correlated to higher ROIC, which came back in the form of higher compensation.

What was most remarkable was that we took a concept that was both powerful and sophisticated and translated it so that it could be understood by every employee in the company. It wasn't something that benefited only senior executives. Every person who works at Dell—from engineers to product managers to our support teams—started thinking about what makes the business profitable and what she could do to improve ROIC.

It's interesting to hear people all across the company who would not otherwise be engaged in discussions about P&Ls or balance sheets, talk and think about the company's ROIC and make decisions accordingly. Rather than think "me," they're thinking "we." It's also helped to reinforce our data-driven culture and reduce ambiguity about how we define value creation in the company. ROIC helps keep our business a meritocracy.

A company of self-reliant "owners" sounds great in theory, but it can be chaos if the goals aren't clear to all. At Dell, it's worked for us because we came up with a consistent strategy and well-articulated objectives:

◆ Look at learning as a necessity, not a luxury. With business moving at such a fast pace, it doesn't take much to get behind in today's marketplace. Today's leaders are voracious learners.

◆ Study the obvious for nonobvious solutions. If you're trying to solve a customer's problem, go and ask him how he'd like to see it solved. This kind of problem-solving "empathy" leads to innovative thinking.

◆ Make failure acceptable as long as it creates learning opportunities. There's no risk in preserving the status quo—but there's no profit, either.

◆ Constantly question—even the good stuff. There's no better way to improve. And don't try to cover up bad news or deny difficult problems. Time is everything—the sooner you deal with an issue, the sooner it's resolved.

◆ Communicate the goals of the organization to everyone. Focus the organization on the customer, not the hierarchy. Encourage your people to do the same.

◆ Treat all employees as owners, even if they technically aren't yet. Once they own what they do, they'll start focusing more on big-picture goals. A sense of pride, balanced with a strong dose of personal investment, works wonders to engender a greater sense of accountability.

Ultimately, our people know that they're what drives the business. They know their success drives the company's success, rather than the other way around. Knowledge brings power, whether it's knowing how a business works or knowing the right way to serve a customer. All of our experimenting and questioning and learning is done in pursuit of one goal: finding the next frontier of value that we can create for our customers.

Giving your people the knowledge, the abilities, and the permission to do what they do best—and take it to the heights of "ownership"—brings more success to a company than anything else I've found.

10

LEARN, DIRECT FROM THE SOURCE

OUR CLOSE CONNECTION TO OUR customers is one of the things we've become best known for at Dell. When I first started the company, that "direct link" distinguished us from our competition; helped us to determine where to best allocate our resources; and allowed us to provide the latest technology, a high-quality product, and great value. To some degree, it still does. But today, customers are becoming ever more aware of their choices—so technology, high quality, and good value are just the price of entry.

The total customer experience—including an emphasis on service and speed—is the next competitive frontier.

We're already seeing it happen. Beyond winning and satisfying your customer, the objective must be to delight your customer—and not just once, but again and again. This leads to true customer loyalty, which sustains your success.

The best way we've found to stay in tune with our customers and keep them happy is to engage in a cooperative, mutually beneficial dialogue. The key is the dialogue—not just talking at, or talking to, your customers, but talking with them—and really listening to what they have to say. When you engage directly with your customers, you begin to develop an intimate understanding of their likes, needs, and priorities. You find out what's working for them—and why. You can try out new ideas on them—ideas worth millions of R&D dollars and countless hours of your people's valuable time—and they'll tell you whether you're on track or not.

Following are the techniques we've developed at Dell, in partnership with our customers, for learning as much as we can from them, in an effort to continually add value to our products and to their businesses. But just collecting and assimilating this information isn't enough. In Chapter Eleven, I'll share with you real-life examples of how we've used this information to gain an edge as a customer-focused company.

KNOW YOUR CUSTOMER'S HISTORY—AS WELL AS YOUR OWN

If the total customer experience is the next competitive frontier, why aren't our competitors all over it?

Good question.

One of the great ironies in business is that while customers are our lifeblood, few companies in most industries bother to take their pulse. Our industry is especially famous for this. The reason? Part history, part habit.

I like to think of the creation of the computer industry as a fable. In the beginning, there were a bunch of brilliant scientists working in laboratories and garages to create an incredible device called a computer, which could do lots of things, from numeric computation to word processing. They worked tirelessly for many years, defining and refining the prototype until finally they had something they were ready to show to the world. Since there was nothing like it, they figured it was worth millions of dollars at least, and customers would feel lucky to actually own one.

We all know how that fable ends.

As oversimplified as it may sound, the course of events depicted in my little fable is what created a technology-oriented industry driven more by the love of scientific invention than by the needs of its customers. That attitude, which was pretty pervasive in the early days, caught on to become a kind of collective habit—and, well, before you knew it, the habit became ingrained in the fundamental structure of the industry. Customers played little, if any, role in the creation of the industry's early products. Computer developers invented great new software and hardware because they could, and the customers who needed technology paid the going rate, whether or not the features really satisfied their needs.

It was a lose-lose proposition. Much of the technology that was created was never purchased. And customers hungry for technology were forced to order from a fixed menu of items, whether they liked it or not, in addition to assuming the high costs associated with funding all sorts of creations.

To make matters even worse, computer companies in those days were vertically integrated—meaning that each computer manufacturer created its own hardware, operating system, and software, contributing to and reinforcing the high prices. As a result, none of these systems worked with one another, making the exchange of information from computer to computer nearly impossible.

This inefficient setup did not last forever, as economies of scale forced the industry to progress from a vertically integrated, closed, proprietary model to a model based on industry standards. The focus in the industry began to shift from high-priced, newly invented technologies that were invented for the sake of being invented, to a range of standard technologies offered at a range of costs.

At last, customers had choice.

DEVELOP PRODUCTS FROM THE CUSTOMER'S POINT OF VIEW

We were really the first personal computer company to organize and build itself around the idea of direct customer feedback. Our attitude was diametrically opposed to the engineering-driven thinking of "Let's invent something and then go push it onto customers who might be willing to buy it." Instead, I founded the company with the intention of creating products and services based on a keen sense of the customer's input and the customer's needs.

Dell entered the computer industry with a new approach that allowed us to deliver great technology at lower cost. By developing and building to order only the systems that our customers wanted when they wanted them, we were able to virtually eliminate the excess cost tied into buying too many components, having to store them, and then selling the surplus at a loss. This enabled us to speed up the process of configuring and delivering our products, saving us time and allowing us to pass on the savings to our customers.

We won and continue to win business on price, but we maintain business relationships by providing high-quality products and the service to go with them.*

The computer industry has come a long way since the era of the closed vertical model, in part because it had to. There was simply no

---

*We've found that pricing is only one-third of our customers' decision-making process; the other two-thirds represent service and support.

way customers would stand for these inefficiencies as the competition grew ever more fierce. Today there are more than 300 million PCs installed around the world, and the vast majority of them can run the same software applications. Because the scale is so large, the applications cost less to buy. Breaking down those proprietary barriers has afforded today's customer lots of choices and a certain level of confidence. He knows that when he buys a PC, he's investing in something that has a wide variety of applications; he's reassured that any training he's had in the past will translate to the new system; and he's free to choose systems from a variety of different manufacturers to run a wide array of applications.

Developing your product or service specifically to fill a customer's need goes well beyond finding out just what customers want to buy and delivering it. It goes beyond providing fair price and high performance. It involves knowing their needs almost before they do.

How do you find that out?

All you have to do is ask.

KNOW YOUR CUSTOMER'S PULSE—BEAT FOR BEAT

A company can't possibly create a great customer experience all by itself. You need to involve your customers intimately in the process.

We do that, fairly easily, thanks to the direct model. The first precept of the direct model is: Know your customers. The second is: Know what they want and don't want, what they like and dislike, and what they value most. The third precept is: Know what you can do to help them be more effective in their business.

We take our customers' pulse regularly—through more than 300,000 telephone, online, and face-to-face interactions every week—and we're constantly humbled by the experience. They've taught us things that have directly affected our success; they've kept us on course and prevented us from doing things that would have been disastrous, like the Olympic project in 1989. And yet one of the most surprising things we learned early on from our customers was that they really valued being asked. There is something about having a direct dialogue with the manufacturer that is more satisfying than being forced to buy what a competitor is selling.* Even more important, we create a relationship that is based on more than just individual transactions. It's based on a continuing exchange of information, enabling us to better serve their needs as we learn more about them.

And that exchange goes both ways. We give our customers information about new products and industry trends that help them maintain their competitive edge. The information they give us tells us which products and services to develop and helps us reinvest our profits with a high degree of precision.

Not all feedback is created equal. To many companies, feedback means anecdotal evidence and comments from which they can feel or sense a trend. But that kind of qualitative feedback is limiting. It's a self-reinforcing question to ask someone whether he is satisfied with the computer he just bought. It's like asking someone if he's smart. You're not going to get a lot of objective—or constructive—feedback. The real answer to the question comes when he buys a second time. Would he buy from you again? Would he recommend your product to his friends? We use aggregate data to sharpen our sense of what customer satisfaction means, and continue to take their pulse many times over the course of our relationship.

We try to take the process one step further. We have defined a series of metrics that define the customer experience in very mea-

---

*The first-ever J.D. Power survey of the computer industry, conducted in 1991, which we won, demonstrated that customers who bought from Dell were more satisfied than those who bought from the conventional dealer channel because they had a way to add their input into the process.

sureable terms; we track the order and delivery process, product reliability, and also service and support from the customer's point of view. Our results are data-driven and based on real-time customer input. And we've designed our business to be flexible enough to respond to those metrics quickly, and to deliver what we believe to be the best customer experience.

The challenge in any business is finding the perfect match between what your customer wants or needs and what you can provide. If you're constantly getting feedback from your customers about what they're buying, what their preferences are, what their needs are, and how well you're doing to meet those needs—and you're willing to listen—you can make the most of the opportunities implicit in those needs.

Customer feedback also helps you benefit from the larger marketplace of ideas. There are hundreds, perhaps thousands, of companies in our business. If one company has a good idea, customers are quick to adopt it. They will say, "Gee, how come you can't do it like these guys?" Those are great learning opportunities.

Nobody has a lock on all the good ideas. The key is the speed of learning and the ability to execute your good ideas. It's not how much you know, but rather how fast you learn, and how open you are to new ideas. Establishing a direct relationship with your customers means that, unless you're not listening, you'll get the best information out there.

BECOME YOUR CUSTOMERS' ADVOCATE

Not surprisingly, different types of customers give us feedback in different ways. We meet face to face with our largest customers on a regular basis, and we have account teams that live and work with them in the field. With small customers and consumers, we create online surveys and real-time focus groups, and have outbound call surveys that solicit feedback. These are things that any company would do.

What's different is how we respond.

We start with the raw data. Every day, literally hundreds of thousands of phone calls, e-mail from the Internet, cards, letters, and faxes come in to our sales and support teams. When a salesperson spends her entire day talking with thirty or forty customers, there's a concentrated solution of customer feedback right there. If a salesperson hears that a lot of customers are asking for Zip drives, then she knows to tell the product manager or team supervisor, and she'll do this in real time. That manager knows to take the salesperson's recommendation seriously, weigh it quickly but carefully, and then figure out how to make it happen.

Our sales and support teams become advocates for our customers. When our product managers are trying to figure out what new features should be in future products, they'll grab a bunch of salespeople, sit down together in a conference room, and say, "What are your customers asking for?" If someone's been hearing for a month how customers are looking for 16-gigabyte hard drives or 24-inch monitors, they'll speak up. Similarly, if a salesperson lost a sale because we didn't have a certain product or something wasn't presented clearly in an ad, she can go over to a product manager and say, "Hey, we'd better get our act together."

The managers and supervisors have learned how valuable this kind of feedback is. In fact, we make serving one customer segment the manager's only job. Why? Because our customer needs are that different. If you just group diverse customers together under one very large umbrella, you can be sure that some of them will not receive the focus they deserve. As a result, we may never get around to understanding that customer's unique needs.

There are lots of cross-functional team meetings within each business group that act on this feedback almost as it occurs. Product managers reside within each of the businesses. Their responsibility is to listen to the sales organization and be in tune with what's going on on a day-to-day basis. Sometimes they even sit side by side with a salesperson and listen to customer calls or go visit customers in the field with our account teams. This way, they're better able to gauge the customers' likes and dislikes for each feature, and are responsible for making the appropriate changes.

The goal is to connect with your customers, collect this information, and use it to cooperate as a partner, all in real time.

EXPLOIT THE "NEXT BEST THING TO MENTAL TELEPATHY"

We like to say that the only communication medium that would be more effective than the Internet is mental telepathy. And the combination of our direct business model and the Internet allows us to take even greater advantage of our relationship with customers.

The Premier Pages are a tool we have developed for more than 35,000 corporate customers to provide them with a direct link into our own technical support and diagnostic databases. They can, of course, order products with a paperless purchase order, but we are going far beyond e-commerce. We have taken our own internally developed support tools and made them available in a customized way to all of our customers over the Internet. Customers are now able to get information on a specific computer system. Because we built and configured these pages to their needs, we can provide their help desks with all the information they need. This results in savings for our customer and for Dell, and, in the end, a stronger customer relationship.

Customers can, for example, link to our manufacturing facilities to find out exactly where their systems are in the build-to-order process. And they can link to overnight carriers through their Premier Page to see where their systems are en route to their business.

We are also able to offer similar services to small businesses and consumers, through Internet-based personalization technology that allows us to keep much better track of individual usage habits and needs. We can then maintain a database of consumer profiles, so when the customer comes online, we can present information that's more in tune with her needs.

If you're a consumer looking for a multimedia system, we can give you the right information based on the individual profile* you completed when you registered. We want to get to the point where if you buy an Inspiron notebook and six months later we develop a new software update, we'll be able to notify you, give you the Web link, and you can automatically download and install it. That's a tremendous savings in time and cost for everyone involved, and about as close to telepathy as it gets.

We recently introduced a self-diagnostic tool on *www.dell.com* that includes hundreds of troubleshooting modules that interactively walk customers through common problems. With an increasing percentage of our support activities going online, customers are clicking on support instead of calling support. That frees our support technicians to work on higher-value activities. Between sales and support, we average almost ten website visits for every phone call at a cost savings of $8 per call.

The key is to shrink the time and resources it takes to meet customers' needs as seamlessly as possible. Creating an electronic two-way flow of information is one way to do it. Another is to do it face to face.

---

*Many customers are concerned about privacy on the Internet. Dell has had a policy since its inception of keeping customers' information private; in other words, we do not sell our mailing lists under any circumstances, no matter whether the customer purchased her system online, by telephone, or by fax. Some companies have privacy policies that mean they will tell you before they give out your information. Our policy is that we will not give away your information, period.

DEFINE A TWO-WAY AGENDA

Our Internet-based communications with customers certainly do not replace the need for face-to-face contact. Rather, the idea is to use the Internet to free up our people to solve more complicated problems and provide even better one-to-one service.

We're always looking for ways to eliminate any friction in the sales and, especially, the support process. One of the keys is understanding what caused a customer to call us in the first place. Could we have designed our product more effectively or made our product easier to set up or use? Could we have sold it in a more effective way, so that this problem would not have had happened? How can we improve the customer experience?

To that end, we have set up a number of forums to ensure the free flow of information with our customers on a constant basis. We arrange technical briefings at briefing centers designed specifically for this purpose at each of our regional headquarters around the world (Limerick, Ireland; Penang, Malaysia; Xiamen, China; Alvorada, Brazil; and Round Rock, Texas). We'll often run two or three briefings every day in each facility. We also have one-on-one meetings in our offices and out in the field.

But one of the most important forums for thoughtful, productive communication with our customers has proven to be our Platinum Councils. These are regional meetings—in Asia-Pacific, Japan, the United States, and Europe—for our largest customers.

These are not the "let's fly you to a resort and bombard you with presentations about why we are so great" style of meetings that have become altogether too common in business, and especially in our industry. Our agenda is quite different.

Dell's Platinum Councils are designed to be genuinely interactive: Customers help set the agenda; our senior technologists lay out our product plans for the next few years and ask for customer input; and there are breakout sessions in which our sales, service, and engineering teams focus on business areas and talk about how to solve problems that may not have much to do with the commercial relationship with Dell. For example, they'll address things like "How do you manage the transition to Windows 2000?" Or, "How do you manage a field force of notebook computers?"

People in businesses as dissimilar as Unilever and Nortel can learn from each other, too, because they share similar problems when it comes to PCs. And we send not only our technologists and salespeople but also people who don't normally spend time talking to customers because they're too busy developing products. All of our senior executives from around the company participate to hear firsthand from the customer how we're doing. The ratio is about one Dell person to one customer.

I spend three days at each of them. They're great events. In the normal course of business, I make sure I have lots of opportunities to talk to customers one on one, but there is something very powerful about gathering customers into a single, truly interactive forum.

Customers really do their homework and come prepared to give us very detailed and thoughtful ideas. At every Platinum Council, we review what they told us last time and what we did about it. We keep an ongoing record of the issues. For example, many years ago, the engineers responsible for our desktops were operating on the theory that customers really wanted very high performance from these products — the faster the better. But what the customers actually said at the Platinum Councils was, "Yeah, performance is important. But if I'm trying to run a bank or an airline, I don't care if the computer is 2 percent faster or 3 percent slower. What I really need is stability—a product that doesn't change from year to year." We responded by designing and building products with intergenerational consistency over many years.

In concept, the idea behind the council meetings is simple. And yet, ideas shared there have become the basis for millions of dollars in savings for our customers—making notebooks with longer-life batteries or loading customers' software for them in our plants—and billions of dollars in new revenues for us.

The Platinum Councils have worked so well that we now sponsor similar conferences for the CIOs of large universities, as well as setting up seminars for other customer segments. It's a way to build an information bridge. We help customers manage technology transitions in ways they might not have considered; they help us understand concerns that might not have shown up on our radar screen. In the process, personal relationships are deepened, so if they're concerned or puzzled about something, they know they can call on us.

REMEMBER THAT ONE SIZE DOESN'T FIT ALL

No matter what your business, it's important to remember that not all customers are exactly the same. By that I mean that their needs, concerns, and expectations run the gamut. And segmentation, when applied to customers, is a strategy that we've used to differentiate among them.

Segmentation brings us closer to our customers. It enables us to understand their needs and operating environment in a deeper way, providing information that is paramount to our company's strategy. The more we segment, the sharper our focus, so that we can tailor products, services, and support specifically to each segment.

A large company, for instance, is most interested in consistency and will trade minor upgrades in speed and performance for stability in its computing platform. It also wants to feel some modicum of control over its PC use across a wide number of users. It seeks consistency and reliability in its network, whether it's a bank or an airline or a law firm.

Consumers, on the other hand, have very different concerns. Consistency isn't as high a priority because a consumer generally has only one computer. What's important to a consumer is having the fastest computer, the latest performance, and the hottest peripherals—like the latest graphics chip, the latest DVD drive, the fastest connection to the Internet.

We've also found that different customers require vastly different levels of service and support. A large company often requires a relatively low volume of support, but support that is very sophisticated and high value-add. When they call us, they want their technical person to speak to ours. For example, one of the biggest issues for the NASDAQ stock exchange is that they have to provide a stock quote within a few milliseconds—and it has to be the same quote on both the East and West Coasts. They *can't* experience technical difficulties! So we have dedicated systems engineers who work onsite with NASDAQ.

That's a very different level of communication from that which is required for an individual consumer, who generally needs higher volumes of support, and support that is clear, but that can most often be delivered easily by one of our service technicians.

Service and support requirements also differ by product. Desktop, notebook, or workstation problems typically occur during the day, when people are using them. Servers, however, are installed in the middle of the night because you can't take them down during the day when people are relying on them. As a matter of course, most server questions come up in the middle of the night, so we provide twenty-four-hour, seven-day-a-week service.

Become aware of your customers' differing needs, and set out to assimilate them into your corporate strategy. The better you can relate, the better your service or product will be received.

TARGET A CUSTOMER OF ONE

The ultimate segmentation is a customer of one, which we offer some of our largest global customers. A Dell account team lives on-site with the customer and focuses on understanding the specific needs of that business—and only that business. And then we tailor our entire product and service delivery strategy to meet its particular needs, almost like aligning our business to mesh with theirs.

We treat these customers as if they were a whole country because, in fact, some of them—like Boeing, Ford, AT&T, and Nortel—are that large. We do this because, as someone at Boeing once said, "We want to be experts at airplanes, not computers."

At Boeing, for example, we have more than thirty Dell people on-site. They provide everything from installation to software imaging, in which we load the machines with the specific software systems necessary to a particular person's job (an engineer has specifically what she needs, while a finance person has only what he needs). We merge peripherals, which means we combine printers and any other equipment and software to go with the computer, provide on-site integration, and take over warranty and service provisions for all PC-related products. We do asset recovery and recycle their excess and/or obsolete units once they are past their useful life. Basically, the things they would have to do themselves or have a reseller do, we do for them. We've become an integral part of their business.

You can extend this personalization strategy beyond your largest customers, too. You simply must decide to take your customers' business needs just as seriously as your own.

At Dell, our focus is not just on trying to be really good at providing value or solving the problem. We dedicate energy to trying to do both. If we can understand what our customers experience when they use our products, we can modify the design or change the manufacturing process to improve their experience overall.

Customers are very vocal—if you're in direct contact with them, and you're listening carefully, you can learn volumes:

◆ Don't be satisfied to know only your own industry. Learn as much as you can about your customers' previous experiences, and not only with your competitors, but with other companies as well. The total customer experience is without boundaries, and the service leaders of tomorrow will cross categories seamlessly, leaving the others behind.

◆ Don't waste precious resources (time, money, energy) guessing at what might work for your customers. In business, there's no glory in creating anything for its own sake. Whether it's technology or tissue paper, develop only what you know your customers really want and need. You'll see customers with greater satisfaction, a decline in costs, and an increase in profitability.

◆ Don't play hard to get. With customers, intimacy is everything. Taking your customers' pulse isn't about making the occasional phone call and asking, "How're we doing?" The closer and more available you are, the more the opportunities for spontaneous learning and the better you can read their minds.

◆ Marry high tech and high touch. Try to keep pace with your customers, and exploit the Internet as a means to achieving that end, particularly in seeking quantitative data. At the same time, create opportunities for good, old-fashioned, face-to-face feedback. Relaxed time with customers, versus overly structured meetings, allows you to learn, since you're listening more than speaking.

◆ Don't forget that customers have different needs, fears, questions, and sensitivities. Tailoring your focus to a customer of one—even if you have many—paves the way for you to provide some personalized attention, while learning as much as you can.

There is no one way to get input that is perfect. But we try to come close. Our job is to take all the technology that's out there and apply it in a useful way to meet our customers' needs. We are devoted to improving the whole user experience—which means delivering the latest relevant technology, making it easy to use, and keeping costs down.

To create a truly virtually integrated organization, you must first go direct to the source—your customers. But that's just the start. Using this information to create high-quality, high-performance products, service, and business solutions must happen next.

DEVELOP A CUSTOMER-FOCUSED PHILOSOPHY

FINDING WAYS TO GET CLOSE TO your customers is critical to your success. But that by itself is not enough. To win as a customer-focused company, you need to use the information you gain to forge a seamless, strategic partnership.

It's the key to integrating virtually.

The whole concept behind virtual integration is to use direct connections, enhanced by technologies like the Internet, to bring your customers virtually *inside* your business so you can meet their needs faster and more efficiently than anyone else.

Many companies focus on partnering with their customers from a single dimension—say, from a marketing perspective or as a sales requirement. We partner with them in every way we can, as our direct relationships with our customers enable us to be simultaneously cost-efficient and customer-responsive. Those relationships have proven to be one of our greatest competitive strengths.

Just how do you do it? You have to be open, flexible, and able to respond to a broad spectrum of customer needs the moment they utter them—if not the moment *before* they utter them.

Following are some of the successful strategies we have developed in cooperation with our customers and as a product of our ongoing dialogue with them. Together, we have worked to improve our businesses on both sides. From saving our customers time and money, and creating solutions that have evolved into best practices— or even whole new businesses—to offering perspective on technology and developing products that are not only right for our customers but right for Dell, the principles behind the lessons we've learned from our customers can be applied to any business or industry.

ADD VALUE "BEYOND THE BOX"

People at Dell often hear me refer to our "best customers," and yet our best customers aren't necessarily the largest, the ones that buy the most from us, or the ones that require little help or service. Our best customers are those we learn the most from, who teach us ways to add value beyond our existing products or services, and who challenge us to come up with solutions that ultimately benefit a range of other customers. In our business, we call this adding value "beyond the box." Our best customers act as leading indicators for where the market is going, and tip us off to ways of improving what we already do well. They raise the bar, encouraging us to continually evolve from a company that sells components of a solution to a company that provides the entire solution.

I remember being in the U.K. once in the late 1980s and visiting one of our customers, British Petroleum in London. The London real estate market at that time was very overheated and space was expensive, yet BP's information technology (IT) guy showed me a whole floor in their headquarters building that they had devoted to configuring PCs. I saw some of their people taking PCs out of the boxes, installing special features, such as job-specific software and network interface cards (NICs) and removing the features they didn't use. I was amazed. Not only was BP spending inordinate amounts of money to configure their machines, but they were also having to do so in high-cost real estate space that they probably could have used for other purposes.

We were watching his people custom-configure these PCs when he asked me, "Do you think you guys could do this for me, so that we don't have to be in the PC business?" I gave it a moment's thought, then replied, "Absolutely, we'd love to do that." What was both expensive and time-consuming for our customer, was relatively easy for us to execute. It also provided a terrific opportunity for us to add the kind of value we knew our customers in other industries would benefit from as well.

At about the same time, Amoco came to us and said, "We're getting all these PCs from you. Can you put a particular NIC in them?" We said, "We've tested our systems with NICs. We've built them for ourselves and installed our own NICs, so, sure, we could do it for you." We set up a special process so that when we built machines for Amoco, we'd automatically add their NIC card. In a fairly simple step, we squeezed more time out of the process; this increased their velocity, enhanced the value of our products, and deepened our relationship with them. It also gave us a terrific idea for building a new business: Dell Plus, which has become a multimillion-dollar program of system integration services.

By spending time with your customers where *they* do business, you can learn more than by bringing them to where *you* do business.

You can experience the issues and challenges they encounter in their daily lives, and better understand how your product ultimately affects the ways in which they serve *their* customers.

The idea of adjusting our manufacturing and product development strategy based on customer input seemed obvious to us, but it didn't appear to be happening with other companies in our industry. When we talked with our customers, they would tell us that our competitors' typical response was, "Thanks for the suggestion. We can't fix that right now, but we'll try to get it in the next time we revise the product." That usually meant in a year or two. In contrast, we try to respond to and assimilate such suggestions into our strategy almost immediately.

EXPAND YOUR RANGE OF VISION

Eastman Chemical, for example, one of our large customers, has its own unique software needs. Some of its applications are licensed from Microsoft, some are programs they've written themselves, some have to do with the way their network works. Normally, they would get their PCs, they would take them out of the box, and then someone from their help desk would come to each employee's desk to hook up the system and load all the software. Typically, this takes an hour or two per computer, and costs several hundred dollars per computer.

Their other option was to buy their computers from a reseller, who would order them from a manufacturer, who would deliver them to the reseller, who would open them up, take out the components they don't want, install the ones they do want, and then load the software and give them to the employees at Eastman. This wasn't exactly the solution Eastman was looking for.

We saw a new opportunity. We created a massive network in our factories around the world with high-speed, 100-megabit Ethernet.

We load Eastman Chemical's software image onto a huge Dell server. Then when a system comes down the assembly line—in any of our manufacturing facilities in the world—it identifies itself over our network as an Eastman Chemical analyst workstation. A few hundred megabytes of data rush through the network and load onto the workstation's hard disk, in a matter of minutes, as part of the continuous flow through our factory.

What happens to the money our customer is saving? They get to keep most of it. We could say, "Well, it costs you $300 to do it, so we'll charge you $250." Instead, we charge significantly less, and we make our product and our service much more valuable. It also means we're not just going to be their PC vendor anymore. We're part of our customer's own information technology group.

Our customers have more important things to do than mess around with personal computers. That's exactly the way you hear them describe it. They say, "We're a bank, we make cars, we run an airline. It doesn't make any sense for us to do these other things. Why can't you do it?"

In our commitment to create the total customer experience, we can and we do. You can, too, by approaching a problem or possible solution holistically, and being willing to look beyond the confines of traditional boundaries to focus on adding as much value as you possibly can.

CREATE OPPORTUNITIES FOR SHARED SAVINGS

A couple of years ago, we started hearing from customers that they were concerned about the total cost of owning and using personal computers. Interestingly, one analyst firm noted that the cost of the hardware totaled only 15 percent to 20 percent of the cost of owning a PC. Even though that figure was debated by other analysts and customers, the issue became a hot topic in the industry.

While acquisition costs are indeed important and do receive a lot of attention, there was an increasing feeling among customers that there were other costs that weren't being managed carefully enough. So we came up with a model that we referred to as "lowest life cycle cost." It covered the cost to the customer of the entire life cycle of the system from getting it to the desk, on the desk, and, eventually, off the desk. We built a computerized modeling program so that a customer could model the combined costs and look for opportunities to save money. The industry has now centered its interest on the total cost of ownership, but it's essentially the same concept that we had introduced two years earlier.

We found that by looking for opportunities that related to creating the total customer experience, we could differentiate ourselves. We were able to use the "lowest life cycle cost" model as an opportunity to show customers the power of our direct business model.

Similarly, over the past few years, several European countries enacted laws requiring computing devices to be recyclable. Making our systems more environmentally friendly has always been a significant concern to us, because we know that if we, as an industry, install 115 million computers per year, at some point, we have to uninstall 115 million computers. But we looked beyond the initial requirement to see whether we could develop a product that both met this environmental need and also provided added efficiencies to Dell.

With this in mind, we challenged our design team to create a new chassis design that was not only totally recyclable but also easier to build and took less time to manufacture and service. Our chassis designs are now fully recyclable; we don't use adhesives or paints, and we took the lead by implementing them not just in those European countries where it was required by law, but all over the world.

This same chassis became an essential tool for lowering total life cycle costs, or cost of ownership. Screws, nuts, and bolts were replaced by simple clips and sliding trays, making it easier for both Dell and our customers' service representatives to access the internal workings. This made for time savings that translated into lower costs for both companies.

An idea that solves our customer's problem—and enhances our bottom line—is a genuine example of win-win for everyone.

BECOME A VALUED ADVISOR

In an average month, a customer might hear about new operating system transitions on the server/workstation side, Intel's latest microprocessor, changes in LCD display technology, as well as the latest development in battery technology and weight for notebook computers. The industry is constantly coming up with improvements in technology, and many of these improvements end up in our products. But it's easy for customers to end up with too much technology—or technology that doesn't meet their needs—if they're not careful.

In acting as our customers' advisor, we try to help them make the right decisions, so that technology actually *adds* value to their business. It's simply a function of looking at our customer's challenges as our challenges. If our customers are challenged by the problem of having to support their PCs, it's not enough to say, "Here's your PC. It's got a manual. Good luck." If we don't take responsibility for their problems, those very same problems will inevitably resurface in some form—most notably, in our losing them as customers.

We try to take responsibility for how our customers' investment is used. We look at the entire value chain of events and ask: How can we help customers manage the complexity of the technology so that it drives their costs down? How can we influence the industry to bring down the cost of this technology?

There's also value for the customer in our discussing future technologies with them. The value of this exchange to us, of course, is clear: Not only do we get an opportunity to try ideas out on them, but we're also testing demand for product features long before the systems will be designed. For the customer, however, this process is helpful to its long-range planning, as access to this early information enables customers to plan for technological change, rather than simply react to it. That's a big issue for our customers these days, because without planning it's impossible to react to the constant array of new technologies. They rely on us to filter for them what they need to know and to work with them to identify exactly what will affect their businesses.

For example, there is a feature in our industry that remotely turns on a computer attached to a network to perform software upgrades, diagnostics, and asset management even while everyone is gone from the office. As with any new feature, different companies offer their own version of this feature before an industry standard is agreed upon. By explaining to our customers what this technology is, we can enable them to make their own informed decision about something that might seem like a good idea but isn't yet supported by the entire industry.

Our key technologists write white papers about emerging new technologies to help educate our customers about important trends in our industry. These white papers help explain to both our customers and our own employees the benefits of ACPI (Advanced Configuration Power Interface) power management, why the Pentium II microprocessor is better than its predecessor, or what features in the latest Microsoft operating system can help customers better manage their PCs.

We'll have our top hardware and software engineers conduct seminars with our most important customers to discuss technology trends forthcoming in the next five years. They describe where the technology is moving and how the standards might be changing. But what's most important to our customers is that our engineers actually recommend when to buy a product in order to extract the most value from it.

That's why we aim to be more than just a computer supplier. We try to become a customer's advisor on technology strategy.

In becoming a valued advisor to your customers, you need to look beyond the product you're selling and seek ways to enhance the total customer experience. It will solidify your bond with your customers to encompass a greater sense of trust, integrity, and partnership, in the truest sense of the words.

HELP SORT THROUGH THE HYPE

Our industry is unfortunately known for a lot of hype and "vaporware"—products that are announced well before they are ready, and sometimes never are. Occasionally, customers are influenced by the press and ask for something that we just aren't excited about developing. And while saying "no" to your customers may seem counterintuitive when you're in the market to sell something, it's actually a very important thing to learn. The reason? Customers appreciate the truth much more than being led down the wrong path, even if it's a path they think looks interesting.

Take pen computing, for example. There was a time when the general consensus among many other computer companies was that pen computing would replace the keyboard as a primary mode of input, especially for mobile computers. IBM, Compaq, Toshiba, and Apple all developed and sold portable pen computers. We, however, did not. One of the companies that developed the software for pen computers sent me one of the devices, and I attempted to give them feedback by writing back to them on it.

It was impossible; the thing simply didn't work.

We went ahead and developed a prototype of the technology simply to show our customers that we could do it, if necessary. In our briefing sessions, we explained where we thought pen computing might fit into the marketplace, and we described the strategy we could have implemented if we had chosen to pursue it. Then we said, "This is an interesting technology but we don't think it's ready yet. If, however, it gets up to speed, there's nothing preventing us from delivering it."

We help steer our customers through the storm of technological options. And our customers help us stay humble. Together, we work to figure out the difference between the next thing and the next *useful* thing.

TURN YOUR CUSTOMERS INTO TEACHERS

In the best partnerships, learning goes both ways. This has always been true for us. As far back as the early days, our customers have helped keep us on track. Our close call with Olympic back in 1989 is a prime example of that. Since then, there have been others, although none so far-reaching.

There have been times when we've been excited about a technology that might very well have turned out to be a big waste of time and effort, if we hadn't checked with our customers first. And there have been times when the computer industry was buzzing about some new development that our customers simply weren't interested in.

I remember in 1991 there was quite a lot of industry excitement about something called the ACE Consortium. Intel had just introduced the 386 microprocessor, and Compaq, Zenith, AST, DEC, and Microsoft all got together and decided that the rival MIPS microprocessor would be perfect for the future of personal computing, and began developing plans to design products based on MIPS chips. We, on the other hand, sat down with a number of our customers and asked them what they thought. Every customer we spoke to said, "Why would we want this?" They were more concerned with protecting their existing investment, so they actually valued the compatibility from one generation to the next much more than we (or any of our competitors) might have anticipated. We concluded that MIPS was not going to afford us any opportunities, and decided not to dedicate resources to it.

I also remember talking to a lot of customers about PC TVs. No one was ever interested enough to convince me that this technology would catch on in a big enough way to actually yield a profit. We had the same experience with television set-top devices. In theory, they may have been great ideas, but for us, not worth pursuing. Our customers simply weren't interested.

It's amazing how few companies in our industry actually create technology with the customers' goals in mind. For example, in 1987, IBM introduced a new product line called the PS/2, which featured a new operating system called the OS/2. IBM claimed the PS/2 boasted greater performance, greater security, and a host of other features. In actual fact, the PS/2 was an attempt by IBM to regain control of the industry through proprietary architecture. But the proprietary architecture didn't offer much in way of customer benefit that was radically different from anything that already existed. The PS/2 precipitated a greater loss of share than it was intended to gain; IBM never recovered its lost share in the PC business. Today, IBM is ranked number six in the United States.

When we've made mistakes—and we've made our share—we have at least benefited from a faster correction because our customer input was more immediate. We often cut our losses before there's a chance for them to develop into bigger problems and make corrections quickly. And we know to cut them off because of the valuable advice we get from our customers.

Jack Welch of General Electric (a Dell customer, we're happy to say) has been quoted as saying, "Everything we do is aimed at either getting a customer or keeping a customer." That's a belief that's always guided Dell, too. I spend about 40 percent of my time with customers. When people hear that, they often say, "Wow—that's a lot of time to spend with customers."

I say, "I thought that was my job."

When you're running a company, or even a group, there are lots of ways to spend your day. But to me, there's nothing more redeeming or refreshing than spending time with customers. I ask lots of questions, like: "Are we doing a good job? How do you like our products? Our service?" If it's a global company that operates in many places around the world, I ask, "How well are we serving you outside this country? Are there opportunities for improvement? Is our team taking good care of you? What are you looking to accomplish in your company that we can help you with?"

Customers know that I'm not looking for insincere praise, or an affirmation of our strengths. They know by the quality of the time that I spend and the kinds of questions that I ask that I want to hear the truth, and that I want to walk away with a list of ideas about how we can work to make a valued partnership that much more significant.

We also try to:

◆ See the big picture. It's not enough to just respond piecemeal to your customers' problems. You've got to be willing to invest in coming up with a solution to the immediate problem *and* look beyond it to see its bigger potential.

◆ Run with the suggestions your customers provide. Ask yourself, "Is this a onetime event, or indicative of a trend? Is this an opportunity ripe for development?" Go even one step further and ask, "Is there another whole business here?"

◆ Always think bottom line—but not just yours. Consider your customers' bottom line as well. Can you save them money, while enhancing your partnership with them? Think strategically about your customers' businesses, and find ways to help them cut costs and increase profits, all the while improving how they can serve *their* customers.

◆ Go beyond selling your products or services, and make yourself valuable to your customers as an advisor. Delivering expert advice with no strings attached does much to demonstrate that you are a trustworthy partner.

◆ Be a student. It's as important to listen as to counsel. Customers can provide a much-needed perspective on products and services you may be too invested in to evaluate objectively. Since they're the ones who'll be buying, it's always better to know sooner rather than later.

Generally speaking, customers have not been particularly pleased by our industry. And yet at Dell, we've always tried to exceed their expectations with our products and service. When you delight your customers—consistently—by offering better products and better services, you create strong loyalty. When you go beyond that to build a meaningful, memorable total experience, you win customers for life.

Our goal, at the end of the day, is for our customers to say, "Dell *is* the smarter way to buy a computer."

FORGE STRONG ALLIANCES

DELL IS VERY MUCH A RELATIONSHIP-oriented company, as you've probably already gathered from the previous chapters devoted to how we communicate and partner with our employees and customers. But our commitment doesn't stop there. Our willingness and ability to partner to achieve our common goals is perhaps seen in its purest form in how we forge strong alliances with our suppliers.

In this chapter, I will share how we at Dell go about creating the strategic partnerships with our suppliers that have enhanced our speed of delivery, allowed us to deliver the latest and best technology, and ensured the highest quality to our customers. You'll also see how something as seemingly simple as clear, frequent communications with them can make a measurable difference in how well you are able to maintain your competitive edge.

Then, in Chapter Thirteen, we'll focus on how we maximize these direct relationships to better realize our potential, in terms of keeping our inventory level down, our time to market rapid, and our quality uncompromised.

As you'd imagine, all the examples found in these two chapters have something to do with technology. Those of you who enjoy hearing about defects per million, megahertz and gigabytes, motherboards, and the like will feel right at home. Those of you who don't, please bear in mind: We're talking about relationships, first and foremost. We're talking about working with those without whom you couldn't survive and thrive.

Technology notwithstanding, I believe you will find that the lessons still apply.

DEFINE YOUR VALUE, TIGHTLY

When you start a company with as little as $1,000, as I did, you spend each dollar very carefully. You learn to be economical, efficient, and prudent. You also learn to only do those things that really add value for your customers and your shareholders. From almost the day Dell was founded, we asked: Should we build components ourselves or have someone else manufacture them to our design specifications?

All the pioneering companies in our industry essentially had to create the components for themselves because they had no choice. They had to become expert in a wide array of parts, simply to get access to the parts they needed. Often, this had little to do with creating value for the customer.

As the industry grew, however, more specialized companies developed to produce specific components. As a small start-up, we didn't have the money to build the components ourselves. But we also asked, "Why should we want to?" Unlike many of our competitors, we actually had an option: to buy components from the specialists, leveraging the investments they had already made and allowing us to focus on what we did best—designing and delivering solutions and systems directly to customers.

In forging these early alliances with suppliers, we created exactly the right strategy for a fast-growing company.

Leveraging our suppliers' expertise has allowed us to scale our business very quickly without having to become an expert in surface-mount technology, semiconductor manufacturing, or building motherboards and other electrical assemblies, all of which would require an enormous commitment of intellectual and monetary capital. It also provides an opportunity to counter conventional wisdom and discover another dimension of value for our customers.

Traditional industry mentality dictates that if you don't build your own components, you'll never have enough control over the process. But by working with outside suppliers, we've found that you actually can gain more control over the quality of your products than if you were to do everything yourself. How? You can choose among the best providers in the world.

You can evaluate and select suppliers that have the greatest levels of expertise, experience, and quality with any particular part. If new processes are developed that push quality levels even higher, you can partner with the firm that has taken advantage of them, rather than being held hostage to the investment you've made in acquiring a supplier.

And if one firm you're working with is having trouble keeping up with the demand, you can pair with others and add additional capacity. By amortizing this risk among a few suppliers, rather than harboring it yourself, you can get what you need faster and more flexibly, enabling you to expand and focus your energies where you really add value.

The goal is to know when you can add value to a process and when you can't. Choose what you want to excel at, and find great partners for the rest.

ALIGN COMPLEMENTARY STRENGTHS
FOR SUCCESS

Customers often say to us, "We don't want to be in the computer business. That's your job. We just want to know that we can get systems, and that they'll be well supported." We feel the same way about disk drives, memory chips, and monitors. Your goal should be to find partners with complementary strengths and a mutual drive for success.

But just because you're partnering with a company doesn't mean your part of that particular job is done. In our case, just because we're not creating the technology doesn't mean that we are leaving things to chance. It's in our relationships with suppliers that the direct model takes on even greater significance.

When we enter into a relationship with a supplier, we share our clear expectations for quality. We then explain what the direct model is and how it can be beneficial to them. We demonstrate that we've created a business system that is extremely efficient at delivering *their* component technology, or product or service to a large and growing market. They, in turn, are usually pretty happy to provide us with their particular technological expertise.

The direct model also affects our suppliers in other ways. Dealing directly with the customer enables us to provide fast feedback to our suppliers—a plus they don't get from other computer companies. Because customers tell us almost immediately what's working for them—or what's not—the supplier is able to benefit and adjust quickly, making appropriate improvements or adjusting output if necessary.

For example, we can see on a daily basis whether customers are shifting their purchases from 17-inch to 19-inch monitors or from CRTs to flat-panel liquid crystal displays. We can also see if this is happening with certain types of customers, or across the market.

Depending on our assessment, we can tell our suppliers that that's where the market is heading. This allows them to align their product mix with customer demand quite rapidly, which, in turn, improves the efficiency and velocity of both their inventory, and ours.

Suppliers tell us that this real-time feedback is invaluable to them in their planning. Traditional business systems couldn't possibly have that kind of pulse on market trends until they had worked through the thirty to fifty days of inventory they have sitting in their distribution channel.

The speed with which our direct approach can get new products to market also helps our suppliers to gain scale and market penetration more quickly with their new technologies. When we began working with Sony, for example, to provide lithium ion batteries for all our notebooks, it was not only a decisively strategic win for us in reentering the notebook market, but was also a strategic win for Sony. When their power technology engineer approached me in Tokyo, Sony knew how to combine lithium ion batteries in the one- or two-cell configurations—but they didn't know what was involved in the ten-cell configurations that a notebook requires. We did. And we gave them access to an enormous market.

We've always promoted the early adoption of relevant technology, like lithium ion. On forty of the last forty introductions of Intel microprocessors, for example, Dell has delivered product in volume on the very same day. Intel chairman Andy Grove likes to say, "Only the paranoid survive."

We think that even the paranoid need friends to survive.

But we have to do our part. We have to stay on top of our customers' needs, and we have to monitor and understand the innovations in the material science world—everything from semiconductors to polymers to liquid crystal displays. We need to track anything having to do with the flow of electrons, and we need to keep asking how these developments might be useful to our customers. Our customers don't come to us and say, "I can't wait to get my hands on some lithium ion batteries." The customer says, "I want a notebook computer that lasts the whole day. I don't want the batteries to run out when I'm on the plane."

It's up to us to effectively translate our customers' desires into relevant technology. This means that we have to be connected enough to those customers and proactive enough in our communications with suppliers to be able to seize the appropriate opportunities.

In a way, I believe that Dell has encouraged the entire industry to become more efficient. By demanding that our supplier partners be extremely efficient at delivering component technology with ever-improving quality, we help suppliers grow, become more effective, and be more competitive. When customers tell us what they want, if we think it's indicative of a larger market or an upcoming trend, we'll ask a supplier to invent it. We also order such high volumes of component technology that our influence can help turn whatever new technology we're using into an industry standard, helping to reduce the cost for all users.

For example, a very high-speed type of memory called synchronous dynamic random access memory (SDRAM) used to be used exclusively in high-powered workstations. As we continued to introduce our Dimension desktops with increasingly more powerful processors and higher levels of performance, customers told us they couldn't fully take advantage of these new performance levels using traditional memory, especially when they were running multimedia applications. So we responded to their feedback and brought the memory and processor suppliers together. The memory supplier modified its architecture to work with the higher-powered processors, and today SDRAM is a standard offering in desktops, although it is about to be overtaken by RDRAMS, which is another standard we helped to promote.

Promoting industry standards—rather than inventing new proprietary technologies to solve customer needs—has really worked well both for us and our suppliers, and has made the market more efficient. Suppose we and a competitor both get disk drives from the same supplier. If the components are based on industry standards, the demand is fungible between one manufacturer and another, providing the supplier with greater flexibility. We benefit because we don't have to pay a premium for the supplier to do something unique for Dell, which also benefits our customers, in terms of cost and compatibility.

With supplier relationships, the sum is greater than the parts. Pairing complementary strengths results in greater efficiency and productivity.

KEEP YOUR RELATIONSHIPS SIMPLE—AND CLOSE BY

Early in Dell's history, we had more than 140 different suppliers providing us with component parts. As we grew, we added new suppliers to keep pace with the massive increases in demand. We soon realized, however, that maintaining these relationships was adding tremendous complexity and cost to our business. There were the costs of designing all the different components into our computers, qualifying them, and testing them. There were the costs of initiating lots of different relationships and supporting them in the field. There were the costs resulting from confusion to our sales and service teams and to our customers. Not to mention the fact that our largest customers were clamoring for the consistency that comes from building stronger relationships with a much smaller number of suppliers.

Today our rule is to keep it simple and have as few partners as possible. Fewer than forty suppliers provide us with about 90 percent of our material needs. Closer partnerships with fewer suppliers is a great way to cut cost and further speed products to market.

Just as you look for a sweet spot in the customer market, try to offer products in the sweet spot of the demand. You might think,

"Okay, to cover 100 percent of market, we might need eight different varieties of a specific component, but we can cover 98 percent of the market with only three." That defines the sweet spot.

The lesson is simple: Complexity kills.

The corollary is equally simple: Proximity pays.

As we expanded around the world, we had to decide whether to optimize our suppliers at a local level or a global level. This is a critical decision for any global company, especially as the world marketplace becomes ever more competitive. At the time, we had many different suppliers for our configuration centers in each country. Of course, there were some regional differences: One country used one kind of monitor, another used another; yet another liked a certain type of disk drive, and a different keyboard.

We came up with the phrase "proximity pays" as a result of translating the ROIC metric down to each component and each supplier. Once we could measure the true returns to our shareholders from buying one component versus another, it was very clear that those suppliers that located their factories close to ours helped us to deliver a higher ROIC than those who were farther away. Obviously, if they were closer to us, we had lower shipping costs. But since component costs decline in value an average of $\frac{1}{2}$ to 1 percent per week, proximity also meant that they could get us products more quickly and we could take full advantage of the component cost reductions.

We went back to our local suppliers and said, "We have a global business and we want you to be a global supplier. We want you to service our factories all over the world. But in order to do so, you must develop the capability to serve Dell all around the world."

And it worked: A vendor who started with us in Ireland knew we were building a manufacturing center in Malaysia, so it set up a plant next to our plant in Penang and then another next to our plant in China. When we recently decided to expand operations in Round Rock, Texas, the same company added a plant there. Next stop: Brazil.

Once you work with a global supplier, inconsistencies resulting from forecasting service and quality levels, from one country and one region to the next, largely disappear. And the process of simplification cuts down on confusion internally, takes time out of the production process, and reduces costs for your customers.

REPLACE THE TRADITIONAL BID-BUY PROCESS

In most business models, the supplier is cut off from the customer by the manufacturer and distributor. The direct model is different. The direct model facilitates and improves supplier efficiency, at least as far as inventory is concerned, as our process of building to customer order depends primarily on our suppliers delivering what we need when we need it. In other words, it's all about buying to order.

When we work with our suppliers, we act as an advocate for the customer who uses our products day in and day out, and experiences success or failure in his own business as a result of things we do or don't accomplish with our suppliers. It's incumbent upon us to see that our partners respond to market demand so that we'll all succeed—and with a freer flow of information going from the customer, through us, to the supplier, there's a much greater chance of that happening.

We spend a lot of time explaining our requirements to our suppliers in terms of quality, design objectives, inventory and logistics, service, global requirements, and cost—although cost as a factor in and of itself is less important than knowing whether a supplier can be competitive over a long period of time.

One of the key attributes we look for in suppliers is flexibility. With our business over 40 percent a year, we are confronted with dramatic increases in demand. Suppliers need to have a sprint capacity to work with us, and our demand can't represent a disproportionate amount of their total capacity.

And they need to invest in themselves to keep up with us.

We'll sit down with our suppliers and say, "Look, our forecast says we're going to need 4.7 million of these now but we might need as many as 5.8 million. What's your production capacity? How long will it take to build a new plant, and do you have the capital to do it? How much of your capacity are we consuming? If the mix changes from 15-inch to 17-inch monitors more quickly than we anticipated or if we need more, how will you deal with that?" Just as we follow three-year plans in our own business, we do three-year capacity plans with our suppliers. That way, we don't end up in a situation where in three years we'll need 18 million of a particular part but our supplier's total capacity is 10 million.

Certainly there are a lot of different ways to deliver computer components. We treat our suppliers as if they're part of our company. We tell them exactly what our daily production requirements are, so it's not "Every two weeks, deliver 10,000 to the warehouse; we'll put them on the shelf, then we'll take them off the shelf a few weeks later." Instead, it's "Tomorrow morning, we need 9,762. Deliver them to door number seven by seven A.M."

Sharing plans and information openly and freely makes a measurable difference. So few companies do this because generally, the buyers are so busy trying to protect themselves that the best the seller can do is fill the order. You can't be a partner if you don't know what your buyer's goals are. You need to replace the traditional "bid-buy" cycle with a relationship based on ongoing communication and a huge amount of shared information.

SET EXPLICIT, DATA-BASED OBJECTIVES

At Dell, we think that our toughest customer is our best customer because the toughest teaches you the most. So it's probably not surprising that we tend to be a tough customer for our suppliers. We are constantly challenging them to reach new heights of quality, efficiency, logistics, and excellence, which helps improve their processes and enhances their success.

One of the tools we use to gauge a supplier's performance is our supplier report card. In it, we set our standards very explicitly: We detail the number of defects per million we will tolerate; we outline what we expect to see in field performance, on our manufacturing lines, in delivery performance and in the ease of doing business with them. Essentially, the supplier report card is a full 360-degree evaluation of our requirements for suppliers. We use it to track an individual supplier's progress against our metrics, as well to compare them with other suppliers who provide similar commodities.

Our goal today is to achieve fewer than 1,000 defects per million on our finished computer systems, although we are continually looking for ways to improve it. What, you may ask, does 1,000 defects per million mean? Say you achieve 99.5 percent of your goal on ten component processes. That's nearly perfect, right? Wrong. When you multiply it out, it only comes to something like 87 percent on the end product. Not so perfect, after all. We set aggressive goals in terms of defects per million for every component because to be able to deliver 1,000 defects per million or less on a PC on a cumulative basis requires exceptional performance from every individual supplier; it means that individual components can only have a defect rate of 0.00001 percent.

We also evaluate suppliers on cost, delivery, availability of technology, inventory velocity, support of our global business, and the ways in which they do business with us over the Internet, which is a terrific tool we use to elevate our alliances to even greater efficiency. And it's not enough to meet our goals on one or two of these objectives; suppliers must support all the key initiatives we are pursuing as a company. We set quantitative measures for success so they know what we expect, and we provide regular progress reports so they know how they're doing. And their reaction has been incredibly positive. They are responsive to the objectivity of the data, which provide them with external metrics of quality control they can apply to their own businesses.

In forging strong alliances with your suppliers, remember to:

◆ Exploit the talents—and investments—of the experts: Ask yourself, can we really afford to devote our people, time, money, and energy into developing whatever it is that you could get from the best supplier in the world? Record companies don't expect their employees to provide the talent, nor do most restaurateurs raise chickens to serve to their customers. Airlines don't make airplanes. Find out where you can add the most value to your customers and shareholders, and find great partners to do the rest.

◆ Keep it simple: Complicated supplier relationships only mean one thing—complications. Fewer suppliers mean fewer opportunities for error, less cost, less confusion, and greater consistency. With suppliers, less really is more.

◆ Keep your friends close, and your suppliers closer: Bringing your suppliers into your business is a hallmark of virtual integration. Keeping them geographically or electronically close results in better service, heightened communication, lower costs, and faster time to market.

◆ Invest in your mutual success: Take the time to communicate your company's goals and strategies to your suppliers. There's no benefit in perpetuating the traditional bid-buy cycle; your supplier can't be a partner if it doesn't know what you're trying to achieve. The challenge is to maintain a healthy level of flexibility and open channels of communication so that suppliers can provide what your customers want and need— and vice versa. Similarly, look for complementary strengths and

management styles to ensure the proper alignment of your
goals.

◆ Be explicit, and be objective: Your quality standards and defect
   tolerance must be detailed clearly at the outset of your
   relationship and consistently throughout it. Use precise metrics
   to gauge how well a supplier is meeting its criteria and to create
   a self-enforcing check and balance system.

One of the most gratifying things in partnering with our suppliers
is seeing just how many have really embraced the ways in which Dell
does things differently. Five or six years ago, it might not have been as
easy to persuade suppliers to adjust their business systems to meet our
needs. But they've seen how the direct model has changed our industry for the better, and how they have benefited as a result, and we've
seen the value-add, both for our customers and our shareholders, that
has evolved out of these strong strategic alliances.

Creating these relationships is instrumental to the success of
your business. But using them to become a source of competitive
advantage is something else altogether.

BRING YOUR PARTNERS
INSIDE YOUR BUSINESS

IN OUR BUSINESS, VIRTUAL INTE-gration—the idea of interweaving distinct businesses so that our partners are treated as if they're inside our company—evolved naturally out of our need to glean ever-better information from our customers and to enhance logistics management with our suppliers.

In Chapter Twelve, I described how we've built stronger, more direct relationships with our suppliers. In this chapter, you'll see how bringing our supplier-partners into our business virtually has become a key component of our success. You'll also see how, in marrying the benefits of a tightly coordinated supply chain with the specialization afforded by our virtual connections, we have created what some are calling "a new model for the information age."

FLIP THE DEMAND/SUPPLY EQUATION

In our industry, if you can get people to think about velocity—how fast inventory is moving, for example—then you can create real value. Why? If I've got six days of inventory and our competitor and his distribution channel have forty, and Intel comes out with a new 700-megahertz chip, I'm going to get that new chip to market thirty-four days sooner. Inventory velocity is one of a handful of key performance measures we watch very closely. It focuses us on working with our suppliers to keep reducing our inventory and increasing our speed.

In teaching suppliers about our business, I've found the greatest challenge is getting them to keep up with our pace. I've also learned, through this experience, that the key to making it work is information. Simple as it sounds, having the right information and ensuring it flows quickly and directly to the people who can act on it enables you to enhance your velocity—either indirectly by improving quality or directly by improving logistics.

When we realized how important reducing inventory was to our success, one of the first things we had to do was try to get suppliers to stop thinking about how much inventory they were going to ship to us. Instead, we had to encourage them to think about how quickly that inventory was going to move from the end of their production line through our manufacturing line and on to the customer. Simply put, we had to change the focus from buying to plan to buying to order (in our case the customer's order); from how much to how fast. And we had to reinvent the traditional supply and demand process to that of demand and supply.

Most of our suppliers were used to the traditional bulk manufacturing strategy of sending large shipments of stuff to a huge warehouse where, more often than not, it would ferment (thereby depreciating in value). Then, when it was needed, PC manufacturers would pull it out of the warehouse. The problem was, not all the inventory was always used, nor was it used quickly enough, resulting in losses for both sides.

The key is in providing your suppliers with all the information they need to make an informed decision. A lot of that has to do with sharing your strategies and goals openly with them. We went to each of our suppliers and said, "Look, here's what our customers are saying they want and need from us. We've figured out a way to meet those needs, but we need your help. Don't send us stuff the way you have in the past. Instead, ship us inventory every day or every hour as we need it. We'll buy from you faster. And if you can do that, we'll buy a whole lot more." The suppliers replied, "You're saying that if we ship you less product more frequently, you'll buy *more?*"

We'd come upon a new way of doing business.

What are the benefits of this model—and demand/supply versus supply/demand—to suppliers? Our demand is consistent and constant. If you average the day-to-day demand of all our customers, it comes out as a steadily increasing straight line of increasing demand. There are no massive spikes from a customer saying, "I want to buy five times more computers at the end of the month than at the beginning." And it prevents "channel stuffing," which goes on all the time in the indirect channel, when manufacturers fill their distribution outlets with products that have aging technologies in order to clear their system for a new product line or to meet quarterly financial objectives. With us, they get a more steady demand and they don't have to shut their factories down for a month to adjust for inventory corrections.

We've found that with your suppliers, in addition to disseminating valuable information as it pertains to your inventory needs (informed, of course, by what your customers are telling you), you need to demonstrate to them how and why it's beneficial to them to deliver materials to you, rather than to some warehouse (as is the norm). The key is to secure the commitment and partnership from your suppliers up front. They've got to believe that it's not just a better way for you to do business, but that there are logistical and bottom-line benefits for their businesses as well. They need to see the added value in delivering based on your need, not a forecast that, however elusive, is also the norm. Only then can you begin to change the process of delivering to suit the customer.

TRADE INFORMATION FOR INVENTORY

The link between the day-to-day demand trend and the incoming material from your suppliers is absolutely crucial to your success—so the shorter you can make the link, the better off you are. Today we have access to technology that greatly facilitates the exchange of this information. We can share methodologies with supplier-partners in ways that just weren't possible five or ten years ago, which results in dramatically faster time to market.

We call this process "trading inventory for information." It's how we've gotten down to just six days of inventory. Speed to market is important for two reasons. One is that it creates competitive value that can be shared between buyer and supplier. The other is that when it comes to delivering the latest product—no matter what it is—you're either quick or you're dead.

We're always looking for ways to reduce inventory further and shorten the time and distance between the end of our supplier's manufacturing line and our customer's front door. To that end, we recently decided not to touch some of our inventory at all.

It sounds incredible, but for us, it made absolute sense.

We have a supplier that makes very good, reliable monitors that we are confident about putting our name on.* We worked hard to get

---

*We can do this with products like monitors that, although they bear the Dell name, aren't made by Dell. This is standard throughout the industry.

them to under 1,000 defects per million, at which point, we decided not to even take them out of the box for testing. At that level of quality, the steps involved in quantity confirmation—shipping them via truck from the supplier to us, unpacking them, touching them, testing them, repackaging them, and then sending them to the end user—would only risk damaging the goods.

So we went to our monitor supplier and said, "We're going to buy 4 or 5 million of these monitors this year. Why don't we just pick them up every day as we need them?" At first, they were confused. After all, we were saying, "If you help us get your product from the end of your line to our customer faster, we won't have any in our warehouse." Given the conventional wisdom, that wasn't a positive thing—so at first, some of our suppliers thought we were crazy. We told our logistics company to pick up 10,000 computers a day from our factory and pick up the corresponding number of monitors from our supplier's factory. Then while we were all asleep, they matched up the computers and the monitors, and delivered them to our customers.

We weren't satisfied doing things the way everyone else did, because that system wasn't working for us. So we came up with our own way of doing things and, with the cooperation of our suppliers, reaped the results. We now do this with a huge variety of hardware, software, and peripherals as well.

Now that our suppliers understand our reasoning, our way of working makes their job dramatically simple. Our orders are typically for thousands of units, and they need to go to only one of six manufacturing centers: Austin, Texas; Nashville, Tennessee; Limerick, Ireland; Penang, Malaysia; Xiamen, China; and Eldorado do Sul, Brazil.

And because we build to our customers' order, typically, with less than five days of lead time, suppliers don't have to worry about sell-through. We only maintain a few days—in some cases, just a few hours—of raw materials on hand. We communicate inventory levels and replenishment needs regularly—with some vendors, hourly—

and we tell them exactly what our production requirements are.

But we don't focus only on increasing our own inventory velocity. We move further down the value chain and help our suppliers increase their velocity, too.

GAIN VELOCITY THROUGHOUT THE SUPPLY CHAIN

Just as the Internet increases customer intimacy, it can also be used to enhance supplier intimacy. The idea is to connect with your suppliers in much the same way you connect with your customers. We use our supplier connections to share inventory data, quality data, and technology plans; to give our partners immediate visibility to the field; and to serve as a central repository for information we all need—which we can access simultaneously, in real time.

Today the whole process of forecasting and resupplying requires human interaction both on our side and on the supplier's side. Given that our factories run on a continuous-flow manufacturing model, we'd like our suppliers to be even more seamlessly linked to us. Our goal is to get to a point where when we use a power supply or disk drive, another one immediately shows up and the supply just keeps replenishing itself, automatically, as we need it.

To do that, we are creating Web-based links for each of our suppliers, just as we did for our customers. These will further facilitate the rapid exchange of information, including component quality as measured by Dell's own metrics and current cost structures, as well as current forecasts and future demand. For example, a Web-based link we designed for Intel allows us to more quickly and efficiently manage order flow and just-in-time delivery of inventory. In that same vein, we're currently conducting pilot programs that will link our internal management systems to suppliers overseas and, ultimately, directly into the very factories that are producing the components.

Plenty of retailers use a similar strategy to reduce their inventory. Wal-Mart, for example, has hundreds of locations stocking thousands of different items, all listed in a complex computerized network so that as soon as a lug wrench is sold in any Wal-Mart around the country, another is immediately sent out to replace it. In a sense, our job is much easier. We want to replace the components as we use them, but with only ten factories in six locations, we work in a much more defined geographic area. By using the Internet to maintain a continuous flow of materials from our suppliers into our factories, our people spend less time placing orders or expediting parts and more time adding value.

The other thing the Internet gives us is immediate transmission of quality data. We have data on product quality that come in every minute of the day. We'd like our suppliers to see the information in real time. If we've given them a goal of 500 defects per million and they're at 750 or 1,000, we don't want to have to wait for a monthly meeting to report customer response. We want them to see it almost as soon as it happens. If we can accelerate the availability of the data, our chances of encouraging suppliers to improve also will increase exponentially.

Closer links also improve inventory velocity. We're down to just six days of inventory on the average; in our European plant, we've actually hit four days. If you're dealing in hours, instead of days, you've got a clearer resolution of the situation. You're also working with a bigger number, providing a greater chance of reducing it.

Of course, you can reach the point where you've achieved most of the opportunity that stands to be gained in reducing inventory. For example, the financial effect of cutting inventory from five to four days is minimal. The real challenge is in continuing growth, market expansion, and product expansion. But if we can increase revenues from $30 billion to $50 billion while retaining inventory at a tight level, that's world-class performance.

By providing real-time information on the day-to-day mix and volume, we can help our suppliers level-load their factories and minimize their level of inventory. By helping our suppliers do a better job of reducing their supply chain lead times and moving to a higher degree of flexibility within their supply base, we can reduce the total cycle time from when we place the order to when they fulfill it.

COLLABORATE ON R&D

The amount invested in research and development has long been a source of pride in the information technology industry. For much of the last decade, it has been looked upon as a leading indicator, not only of the value of your company, but also of its future. At Dell, we've realized that what your research and development delivers, in increased value to customers, is far more important than the actual amount of money you spend.

More than $12 billion is spent in our industry every year on research and development of computer systems and related technologies. A little more than half of that is spent by Microsoft and Intel; the rest is distributed among literally hundreds of different companies.

We spend about a third of a billion dollars and employ some 2,500 people to research and develop technologies that meet our customers' needs. (This does not include our investments in technologies like the Internet, which have helped transform our business processes.)

For that investment, we've delivered products that have continued to beat those of our competitors — some of whom spend much more — in terms of reviews (by technology press and industry analysts) and, more importantly, in terms of market demand. That's because we weigh our options very carefully, as far as what we decide to make or buy. We choose deliberately when to influence others to improve their existing technologies, and when to create technologies ourselves. As with nearly every other decision we make at Dell, we are guided by what will provide the best value-add to our customers.

To decide what we should make and what we should buy, we apply the test of general market availability. If something is generally available from a wide variety of sources, that suggests that it's not too hard to develop. We can't create much value for our customers by developing something that's already available. Whenever possible, we want to be first with relevant technology, and we want to be best. Otherwise, there's little chance of a significant return.

Take the late 1980s, for example, when many PC companies were developing video chips. IBM was developing its own video chips for its PCs, Compaq was developing its own video chips for its PCs, and about twenty start-ups were also developing video chips for other PCs. We had a choice. We could either enter the race as the twenty-first horse and try to out-engineer all the start-ups *and* Compaq *and* IBM, or we could spend our time and engineering talent figuring out which company would come up with the best video chips and partner with them to produce the best product and solution.

Some might have seen our lack of investment in internally developed video silicon as a strategic error. Others might view this choice as just a marketing or procurement exercise. We saw it as an engineering exercise. We were willing to invest our engineering expertise evaluating the different companies and products, then help our chosen partner by providing input, ideas, specifications, and talent so that we could both succeed.

Sure, we could have hired a world-class team and developed a winning video chip ourselves. But would we have gotten a return on our investment that was commensurate with our company's objectives—and that we could sustain over time? There's a substantial element of risk at stake when you enter or continue to pursue activities you shouldn't be pursuing. It's not simply a question of where you can get the best return on your capital, but also a question of focus.

By understanding the drivers of value and where value is created, you can make the right decision about when to partner and when to do things yourselves.

CONSIDER THE CUSTOMER'S WORKING ENVIRONMENT

One of the most important things we do is to try to recognize when we can influence our technology partners to refine or change their products to improve our customer's overall experience with our products—not in a laboratory or in a manufacturing plant—but in the customer's own working environment.

That's why a significant amount of the R&D we do is software-related. We focus on making the installation and setup processes easier, configuring machines for many different languages, enhancing systems management, and helping customers create customized software images, so that their machines arrive in a ready-to-use form. It doesn't matter how technically proficient our customers are—they have better things to do than spend their time configuring their PCs.

Take Microsoft's Windows 98 operating system, for example. Since Dell's systems are built-to-customer order, there are literally thousands of possible combinations for peripherals. To make sure the software is set up to run with the customer's own unique configuration used to mean that the customer had to spend between thirty and forty-five minutes navigating the software setup process for her Dell computer.

Here was a situation where we knew we could add real value. We didn't want our customers to have to work that hard. So we worked together with Microsoft to insert some software code we developed that recognizes a massive number of combinations of peripheral devices, languages, and system components. We could then complete and test all the installations in our factories and reseal the operating system software. This has reduced our customers' setup time to between two and three minutes.

But sometimes it's not enough to partner with our suppliers to solve customer problems. Sometimes we decide that the best way we can reach this goal is to do the majority of the design work ourselves. One of the key problems that many of our corporate server customers face is the physical space required for the massive cabinets that house multiple servers mounted in racks. This may sound like a very basic issue, but the engineering expertise needed to solve this problem was anything but ordinary. To reduce the amount of space needed for servers in the rack-mount meant that we had to reduce the size of the server itself. The powerful processors and disk drives used in servers also generate a lot of heat, which meant that we had to figure out a way to cool the motherboard because the processors and other components didn't have the airflow of a larger space.

Our server design team went to our portables engineers and said, "Maybe we can work together to apply the miniaturization and cooling technology that you've become expert with in notebooks to design a smaller server motherboard." The result was the industry's first "4U" rack-mounted, four-processor server using Intel's Xeon Pentium II processors, which provided the means to house ten individual, high-end servers featuring four processors each, in the same amount of cabinet space that used to be required for just two or three servers.

The Internet makes the connections between our own design teams, and with our technology partners, even more intimate. An engineer sitting at Dell, an engineer at a plastics supplier, and an engineer at a company that assembles electronic circuit boards that we designed can share the same design database and set of notes even though they might be separated by a dozen time zones. The teams may not all be working in the same company physically, but they're working together virtually—on the same project, from the same set of specifications and metrics—thanks to the Internet.

By working with our partners as if they were part of our own design team, we forge an unbeatable alliance. We share product road maps, test our new products with theirs, and explain what features are important to their being first to take those technologies to market. They assign their engineers to our design team, and when we launch a new product, their engineers are stationed right in our plants. If a customer calls in with a problem, we have the ability to check it out almost instantly and, if necessary, refine or make adjustments in real time. It's not a conventional buy/sell relationship. It's not, "Here's what we have to sell—do you want it?" It's more like, "Here's what we need to accomplish. Let's find a way to get there together."

CAPITALIZE ON THE CRITICAL LINK

Our suppliers are usually willing to go all out for us because we offer them a crisp understanding of the market and what customers are willing to pay for. When we tell our suppliers, "We think this particular technology will be a hot one," we get their support. Or if we say, "Our customers are asking for this particular technology, can you make it?" they do. We provide the critical link between our suppliers and our customers through the direct model.

The direct model allows us to take product ideas and technology ideas and merge them firsthand with customer reactions and requirements to help refine our product plans and give feedback to technology suppliers. Most companies are actually not as connected with customers as they think they are or as they would like to be. As a result of our intimate relationships with our customers, our suppliers actually hear stuff from us that they would otherwise have little or no access to.

And sometimes the simplest things can go a long way to improving the quality experience and the cost for our customers. We once had a problem with customers calling to complain that their monitors didn't work. But when the monitors were sent back to us and we plugged them in and ran multiple tests, they worked just fine. After a fair amount of research, we figured out what the problem was.

The adjustments for the monitor were difficult to access, and when the screen was lit, it was difficult to set the parameters for contrast or viewable dimensions. In either case, the customer was, for good reason, irritated. And the cost of shipping monitors back and forth was expensive for everyone.

So we brought our supplier to our headquarters. They listened in on the conversations our technical support people had with our customers. They brought their own technical support people, and helped to train ours. And by our mutual efforts, we realized that a software enhancement and a different placement of the monitor controls would fix the problem. Our warranty costs for monitor returns were reduced by 40 percent.

If you hope only to react to your suppliers, or to the industry forces around you, you will, at best, get only the market standard, which is exactly what your competitors are getting. If, however, you can work with your suppliers and technology partners to provide meaningful input in their designs, you've got a powerful relationship. Here's how:

◆ Don't underestimate the value of information: Managers at every level within all good companies today know there's a fundamental need to communicate. But there's a real difference between simply sharing information and using it to reinvent your relationships. In a virtually integrated business model, the quality and relevance of your communication — your data — can be more important than your physical assets.

◆ Communicate directly with decision-makers: Talking candidly — and directly — with your suppliers is as crucial to the health and wealth of your business as communicating with your people and your customers. Don't relegate them to "behind the scenes" status. Your competitive edge in the marketplace depends largely on how effectively and how quickly your suppliers can provide what it is that you sell to your customers.

◆ Flip the equation: Don't settle for the standard supply/demand relationship—it doesn't work anymore. Work toward demand/supply. The benefits to both sides, in terms of time, market flexibility, cost-savings, and competitive advantage are immeasurable.

◆ Think real-time: Get beyond just-in-time—surplus time can make the difference between being quick and being dead. A heightened level of communication with suppliers will enable you to get exactly what you need, when you need it. A little too late is just too late in most businesses today.

◆ Differentiate with your R&D dollars: More is not necessarily more—nor is bigger always better. Your R&D must really deliver some tangible value-add to your customers, or it's not R&D—it's wasted time and money. Rather than invest it in common "soon to be commoditized" goods, spend it on the development of products and services that will serve as differentiators to your overall competitive strategy.

◆ Get on line. The speed with which invaluable feedback is communicated contributes to a greater connection between teams of people working toward the same goal, regardless of where in the world they are physically located.

By treating our suppliers as if they were a part of Dell, by sharing information on everything from customer feedback on product features to inventory management practices, we all win. Leveraging our collective strengths sharpens everyone's competitive edge.

DIFFERENTIATE FOR
A COMPETITIVE EDGE

EVER SINCE DELL BECAME A SERIOUS contender for market share in the computer industry, people have asked how we deal with our competition. The short answer is: When you've got only single-digit market share—and you're competing with the big boys—you either differentiate or die.

Differentiation, as a strategy, should be common sense when you're seeking to create and maintain a competitive advantage. But often it's not. Whether or not they know it, many companies unwittingly adopt strategies that are merely slight variations of their competitors'.

Throughout this book, I've described some of the key differentiators that have contributed to Dell's success—such as providing superior customer service, achieving high velocity on inventory and in getting new generations of products to market, focusing on the total customer experience, and, of course, the direct model itself, which gives us intimate knowledge of customer wants and supplier capabilities. Based on my experience as a manager and strategist at Dell, here are some principles and strategies for creating differentiators in your own field or industry.

FOCUS ON YOUR CUSTOMERS, NOT YOUR COMPETITION

Lots of companies get so caught up in what their competition is doing that they spend more time looking over their shoulders than looking ahead. Focusing all your energies on what your competition is doing simply means that you're overlooking your greatest source of competitive advantage: your customers. Companies that are successful today—and, perhaps more importantly, companies that will be successful tomorrow—are those that can get closest to their customers' needs.

When I founded the company on the idea of designing and selling custom-made computers directly to end users, bypassing the dominant method of computer distribution, I wasn't deterred by the fact that for as long as the computer industry had existed, the competition had always sold mass-produced computers indirectly through a dealer or distributor channel. I was actually energized by the opportunity this new way of doing business represented. Even though what we were doing was unprecedented, we had the reassurance of customers telling us exactly what products and features they wanted. Our approach worked, not because we were the only company doing it, but because we were the only company obsessed with serving the needs of our customers—in terms of quality, speed, and service.

Because dealing direct is such an advantage, we knew at some point that our competitors would try again (as many had ten years ago) to copy us. In 1997, soon after Steve Jobs took over at the ailing Apple Computer, he held a rally to announce that Apple was going to come after Dell by selling direct. Around the same time, Compaq and IBM announced that they, too, would start to sell direct.

We reacted by continuing to do what we always have: focusing on the customer, and not on the competition. When our indirect competitors declared that they would go direct, they found themselves acknowledging the superiority of our system in working with customers. It's certainly gratifying to see a competitor's approach validate your success, and in our case, I believe it's helping to accelerate the transition from the old business model (indirect) to the new (direct).

Thanks to the intimate information we are constantly soliciting from our customers and suppliers, we can actually choose on an ongoing basis which products and services to offer at any given time, and which hold the most value for our customers. That allows us to choose not only which customers to market them to but also which companies we want to compete against.

PLAY JUDO WITH THE COMPETITION

To compete successfully in any industry, you must first understand its fundamental economics, which can reveal new customer opportunities, products, and services. If you are starting or running a business, and you choose to leave the economics until last, you won't actually be capable of developing the customers and product strategies that will be necessary to achieve balanced success, which I define as growth of market share (or revenue), profitability, and liquidity (or cash flow).

Understanding the profit pool of your industry—where your competitors really make money—can open your eyes to new opportunities. Think of a competitor that has high market share and is very profitable in a specific part of the market. Then think about how compelling it would be to exploit that strength as a weakness. Your competitor will most likely not be able to respond to an aggressive attack without significantly reducing its profit.

We call that playing judo with the competition.

Here's an example. In the mid–1990s, it became clear to us that some of our competitors were earning more than half their profits in servers. Furthermore, their servers, while good products, were onerously and unjustifiably priced to subsidize other less profitable parts of their business. By pricing servers so astronomically high, they were practically exposing their vulnerability, while passing extra costs on to some of their best customers. What emerged was an incredible opportunity to disable our competitors' ability to gouge the market, while at the same time to grow our business in servers.

In September 1996, Dell introduced a new line of servers at very competitive prices. The market exploded. This aggressive launch reestablished our presence in the server market, a market in which we are now number two worldwide with over 15 percent market share; by draining our competitors' profit pool, we also weakened their ability to price as competitively in other markets, such as notebooks and desktops, where we also compete with them.

In fact, we had done the same thing with desktops seven years earlier—accompanied by the usual commentary from our competitors, who said it couldn't be done. And it's since happened again with workstations and storage products.

We didn't move into the workstation market until a year after other major competitors did. But within nine months, we became number one in the United States and number two in the world. Rather than rushing in to be first, we took the time to evaluate the opportunity carefully, figure out the optimal strategy, and be best.

The Internet also affords another great example of how to play judo with the competition. For Dell, the Internet is the ultimate extension of the direct model. And yet for many of our indirect competitors, it's a real lose-lose proposition. Sure, they're talking about how they will attempt to go direct and copy our business model, but many have already tried in the last ten years, unsuccessfully. And for them, dealing direct is the ultimate channel conflict. They've built their business on the traditional channel of distributors, dealers, and resellers, rather than on direct relationships with customers. By engaging in a direct dialogue with an end user, an indirect manufacturer is going into competition with its reseller, who still sells the vast majority of their products today.

That only draws more attention to Dell faster. If a customer is thinking of buying direct from a manufacturer, what better way to do that than go to the company that is the leader in selling direct?*

TURN DISADVANTAGE INTO PROFIT

Turning a perceived disadvantage into an advantage is another form of playing judo with the competition, and another way we've sought to sharpen our competitive edge.

Back in the 1980s, when PC sales really began taking off, getting your computer serviced was about as enticing—and involved—as having a root canal. If you bought the machine at a computer dealer, you had to put it into the car and drive it over to the service center, where you would wait in line to drop it off and come back days, maybe weeks later.

And then there was no guarantee it could—or would—actually be fixed.

When I first founded Dell, prospective customers initially had a hard time imagining buying a computer over the phone because they

---

*Especially since many of the indirect companies that are claiming to go direct are not actually able to provide product that way.

assumed that servicing it would be impossible. Without a store to drive it to, they figured they'd have to box it up, mail it in, and then wait even longer to get it back. Then of course there was the fear that, because a computer was an expensive proposition to begin with, sending it in the mail would pose an even greater opportunity for damage (not to mention the shipping cost).

Competitors also assumed that because Dell sold direct to customers, we would not be able to create an advantage in service. With the added "benefit" of resellers and physical stores, they assumed they would always have an advantage in service, however bad theirs might be.

They were clearly wrong.

From the very beginning, we saw a huge opportunity to provide extraordinary service where our competitors saw none—and designated it one of the company's early objectives. In 1986, we offered the very first program in our industry for on-site service—a kind of "house call" service for sick computers. If your computer had a problem, you didn't have to go anywhere; we came to you—to your business, house, or hotel room. And we would come by the very next business day or on the same day.*

Suddenly, our competitors' service centers looked a little old-fashioned—and really slow. Even today, if you take your computer to be serviced at a retail service center, the repair time can be as much as two weeks, a far cry from the next business day. And there's still no guarantee that it will be fixed. What the competition initially assumed would be a disadvantage for us turned out to be a massive advantage.

Global expansion afforded another case of turning a disadvantage inside out. In the mid–1980s, when we were looking to expand

---

*Later we broadened this service to include two-hour and four-hour on-site service.

into the U.K., we became aware of a company called Amstrad, which was an early leader in the PC business in the U.K. market. Amstrad was well known for selling what was essentially a disposable PC—a very inexpensive machine with a high failure rate and little support from the company. Nevertheless, in the absence of any real competition, they sold an unbelievable number of them—which created a terrific opportunity for us.

How? In selling cheap, unreliable computers that were not well supported, Amstrad essentially taught a very large number of consumers in the U.K. a memorable lesson: Never buy a low-end PC with unreliable components and lousy support. It also created a market of knowledgeable, however disillusioned, PC users, who were predisposed to buying more sophisticated systems from a company that backed them with great support and service—even if that company did not have the initial advantage of entrenched market share. Fortunately for us, Amstrad misunderstood its market, laying the foundation for the enormous growth and success that Dell has experienced in the U.K. And because our U.K. operation was our first move outside the United States, it served as a springboard for our success globally.

We've even gone so far as to seek opportunity in a lawsuit. Early in our existence, one of our competitors sued Dell for claims we made in advertising. But their strategy for winning back their reputation—and presumably their customers—actually backfired. Because of the press surrounding the suit and our competitor's overreaction to our advertising, their customers started wondering if perhaps there wasn't some truth to our claims for equivalent or better performance at lower prices. In the end, the suit created more attention for our company and gave us exposure we could never have purchased on our own. And because they were the gold standard at the time, our competitor lent credibility and interest to Dell in market segments where it hadn't existed before, which increased our momentum.

Where others see a disadvantage, look for profit.

FIND YOUR EDGE IN EXECUTION

Some businesses are founded on the idea of the silver bullet—one almighty product or patent that sits in a safe, guarded place twenty-four hours a day. But that's not where growth is coming from in today's—or tomorrow's—economy. The key is not so much one great idea or patent as it is the execution and implementation of a great strategy.

Look at Disney or Wal-Mart or Coke. You can understand their strategy—it's really not that complicated. But it's genius! It's completely comprehensible, yet few companies can really replicate their success.

Why? It's all about knowledge and execution.

Traditionally, it was thought that lack of capital was the barrier to entry into a new competitive market. Take a look around, and you'll see that's just not true anymore. Information will increasingly become both a tool to help businesses hone their competitive edge and a weapon to protect them against the competition.

Besides Dell, there are countless successful companies that are thriving now despite the fact that they started with little more than passion and a good idea. There are also many that failed, for the very same reason. The difference is that the thriving companies gathered the knowledge that gave them a substantial edge over their competition, which they then used to improve their execution, whatever their product or service. Those that didn't simply didn't make it.

Our epiphany about execution came, for many of our people, from the weekly Customer Advocate Meetings held in the early days of the company's history.

In these meetings, salespeople served as "advocates" for their customers who had issues with Dell by sharing the issues with a larger group of employees from many different functions within the company. Actions were assigned on the spot to correct any processes that might be affecting customer satisfaction. If you attended this meeting regularly, you soon noticed a pattern: Almost all the complaints were about what the industry deems "little things," like whether the power cord was in the box, whether the box was designed for easy access, or whether it was delivered when we said it would be. We began to realize that customers were less focused on what the industry calls "big things"—such as product features or hot technology—probably because those needs had been largely satisfied. We were fascinated to learn how the "little things" became "big things" to the people who really mattered.

If we had adopted the prevailing industry mentality, we would have said, "On-time delivery, provision of service, spare parts, all those things are the responsibility of the dealer. Our job is manufacturing, technology, and all the fancy stuff." But in deciding to deal direct, we had opted to be responsible for anything and everything that affected our customers' experience—especially the little things.

By and large, the computer industry's ability to deliver a spare part by the next business day is pretty bad. Everyone accepts it, bad as it may be. But what if FedEx delivered packages by the next business day only 90 percent of the time? Would they have been successful? Of course not. Rather than look to our competition to set the standard, we look to companies in other industries, like FedEx, who excel at execution and who share our goal of providing an extraordinary customer experience.

SET STRETCH GOALS

Resting on your laurels—no matter how much you've accomplished—is a sign of trouble. It's easy, when things are good, to assume that you're invincible. But that's exactly when you're weakest. That's when people stop looking for innovations and new opportunities, and when your competition is most likely to play judo with you.

The way we've successfully maintained our edge is by setting stretch goals for ourselves. They're not your basic "Let's strive to improve by 20 percent" goals; they're big. For example, in 1997, we came up with the goal to sell 50 percent of our systems over *www.dell.com* within the next few years. Since we were at that time selling $1 million per day online (and our annual revenues were about $12 billion), this seemed, on the face of it, like a hugely aggressive goal. But we didn't just pick a number out of thin air; we carefully calculated overall market growth, the potential for the market to buy online, and the potential market for our products. We didn't pick the low end of our calculations, either. Nor did we expect to achieve our goal in isolation. We pulled together as a company, to be sure, but we brought our customers and suppliers into the mix as well, and took it to the next level as a virtual team.

By the fall of the following year, we had already achieved more than 20 percent of our annual revenues through sales over *www.dell.com*. Our competition didn't know what hit them; our people felt unstoppable. Rather than feeling like packing up and going home, they were pumped to conquer the next goal.

In coming up with strategies to beat your competition, consider your core strengths. Then dial it up a few notches. Set a clearly communicated goal, and rally your people around it. Encourage them to ask, "What do we need to change to do that?" Make them take a step back and think outside their functional discipline. They might think, "I could make this goal if someone in this other group would also do things a little differently." In a business where there are few established norms, you need to take more risks. That doesn't mean you should be reckless. As our company has grown, the risks we've taken have diminished in intensity because we have a better sense of what innovations and experiments have lead to our success.

Experimentation begets competitive advantage. Once you've systematized a way of encouraging experimentation in your people, they will start looking on their own for ways to drive improvement.

SKATE AHEAD OF THE COMPETITION

Sometimes the best defense is a good offense. The great hockey player Wayne Gretzky once explained his success by saying that he didn't skate to where the puck was, he skated to where the puck was going to be. We try to stay nimble and alert so that by the time our competitors have to moved to where we were, we're already somewhere else: somewhere stronger and more strategically positioned for even greater success.

To get to where the puck's going to be, you have to think about the change elements that exist in business: changes in customers' buying behavior, in technology, in the existing competition, in potential competition, and the most fundamental change of all, in what your business is doing that can be done in a different way. There's a saying in the technology field that what can be done, will be done. If something can be improved, someone will figure out a way to do it. No matter what your business, that someone had better be you.

We try to create these changes. We've helped drive customers to buy computers over the Internet and in so doing have changed the nature of Internet commerce in our business. But if Dell hadn't anticipated that change, we would have left ourselves vulnerable to a competitor who did.

In a world in which technological change occurs at a faster and faster rate, the customer will have a much greater say in defining future products. Because of the Internet, the existence of a specific physical location will become increasingly less relevant, and the ability to see all the cards, face up on the table, will provide consumers with an incomparable opportunity to evaluate products and prices instantaneously. In a transparent market such as this, the assets of the past can quickly become a liability.

You must always be aware of the elements that are changing the competitive landscape in your business, and try to anticipate them before they happen.

Something wonderful occurs in your business when a critical mass of people understand these fundamental concepts and are able to build on them and refine them rapidly. There's almost an exponential growth of learning. The buildup of knowledge and expertise in your company can provide a considerable competitive advantage in the new economy.

Just how do you differentiate in order to hone your competitive edge?

◆ Think about the customer, not the competition: Competitors represent your industry's past, as, over the years, collective habits become ingrained. Customers are your future, representing new opportunities, ideas, and avenues for growth.

◆ Work to maintain a healthy sense of urgency and crisis: This doesn't mean that you want to fabricate deadlines or keep people so stressed that they quickly burn out. Set the bar slightly higher than you normally would, so that your people can achieve aggressive goals by working smarter.

◆ Turn your competition's greatest strength into a weakness: Much as every great athlete has an Achilles' heel, so, too, do all great companies. Study the competition's "game": Exploit its weakness by exposing its greatest strength.

◆ Be opportunistic, but also be fast: Look to find opportunity, especially when it isn't readily apparent. Focusing on the customer doesn't mean that you should ignore the competition. If something that your competition did or didn't do provided you with an opportunity today, would you recognize it and be able to act on it immediately? Today a competitive win can be decided literally one day at a time. You have to act fast, be ready, then be ready to change—fast.

◆ Swing for hits, not home runs: Business is like baseball. Go for
the highest batting average rather than trying to hit a home run
every time. If your competitor is batting .300, you want to bat
.350 or .400. No one's batting 1.000, so you can't worry about
it. What you want to focus on is being the best as often as you
can. Because there's no such thing as a grand slam product or
technology that lasts forever, your competitive edge must come
from strategic execution, and from gaining knowledge,
studying the economics of your business, and ensuring the flow
of information throughout your organization.

◆ Be the hunter, not the hunted: Success is a dangerous thing, as
we are at once invincible and vulnerable. Always strive to keep
your team focused on growing the business and on winning
and acquiring new business. Even though your company may
be leading the market, you never want your people to act as
though you are. That leads to complacency, and complacency
kills. Encourage people to think, "This is good. This worked.
Now how can we take what we've proven and use it to win new
business?" There's a big difference between asking that and
asking, "How can we defend our existing accounts?"

When you compare Dell to its channel competitors—retailers or
resellers who sell to companies—we believe we have a number of
profound competitive advantages. We actually manufacture our own
products, so we know more about them than any reseller does about
what's in his store. We talk to real technology planners inside companies, as opposed to dealing only with a procurement group. Our
support is advantaged; we can go back to our engineering team to ask
for changes and better information.

Our business model gives us a more efficient, healthier economic engine, which allows us to invest in sophisticated systems and

support, and to hire and train the best people. A lot of resellers are struggling right now because their manufacturers are squeezing the margins so hard that there's no way for them to earn a decent profit. So they can't hire and train great people. Because they are squeezed so much by the indirect manufacturers, they can't expand geographically, so they can't compete with us on a global basis. If you take a look around, you'll realize that there's no such a thing as a global reseller.

The indirect channel is perpetually playing defense to our offense.

The ultimate test for Dell will be how well we do in the face of our competitors changing their business model while we further extend our direct model and continue to expand. Will they find ways of making improvements to what we've defined as our signature differentiator?

Only time will tell.

THRIVE ON CHANGE IN
THE CONNECTED ECONOMY

WHEREVER I GO, WHETHER I'M GIVING speeches or talking to customers, I'm always asked lots of questions about e-commerce and the future of business. No matter who the audience, one simple question is asked again and again:

What happens next?

The high-tech industry is particularly known for its volatility—but today businesses in other industries are far from immune. The pervasive use of technology throughout businesses large and small, and the furious rate at which information is exchanged, have increasingly made the need to embrace change an important factor in any business's success.

Change no longer represents the occasional need to react to far-reaching trends or industry influences. It's more like the Chinese character for crisis, which represents both danger and opportunity. Change *is* opportunity. It is also constant, direct, and temporary, for once things change, you can bet they're going to change again.

Learning to thrive on constant change is the next frontier.

FIND OPPORTUNITY IN AN AGE OF UNCERTAINTY

At Dell, we never talk about "managing change" or "dealing with change" because change is all we've ever known. Dealing with change implies that change is an occasional nuisance that can be handled or contained, which is simply not the case. The key to finding opportunity in an age of change is to embrace it wholeheartedly.

Many companies are justifiably afraid of change. When you assume that things are "as good as they can be," the concept of change can only appear negative, threatening to the status quo. Companies spend countless precious hours and dollars on crisis management, attempting to contain and/or minimize change, without ever considering that *the very thing they fear could be the best thing that ever happened to them*.

We dive headfirst into change. Part of that is because it's all we've ever known, but it's also because today, it's a must. When you're dealing direct, there's no place to hide from change. Nor should you want to, as change promotes growth. We've seen, for example, that our willingness to constantly reassess and adapt our direct-model strategy affords us the opportunity to grow much faster than the market we're in. And yet the larger you become, the more difficult it is to add the people, the infrastructure, and the facilities to keep up with that growth. So while it may seem counterintuitive, a lot of our time is spent planning and preparing for change, projecting and encouraging people to look forward to it and see it for the opportunities it provides.

Planning for and communicating clearly the opportunities

implicit in a changing marketplace or in changing customer needs is the way to encourage employees to embrace change without fear. And it will allow you to create a cooperative approach to change, where everyone knows what they need to do, as well as deliberately build a healthy dose of ambiguity into your organization, so that it can grow, evolve dynamically, and adapt accordingly at its own pace.

Learning to thrive on change does more than just grow your business. Beyond teaching your people to respond to crises faster, it encourages them to look for new opportunities by expanding their imaginations. In so doing, it elevates your ability to embrace change to a competitive strategy.

Expect to live in a flexible, dynamic, fast-moving environment that is the norm, rather than the exception. To thrive on change, you must understand how to give in to it, flow with it, and derive strength from it.

There's no other way.

TAP INTO THE POWER OF THE INTERNET

Change was traditionally one of those squishy, amorphous business buzzwords, like culture and teamwork, that people talked about a lot without really knowing what they were saying.

What's changed? Everything.

Take the Internet. It is one of the most powerful catalysts for changing the face of business this century. Thanks to the Internet, the amount of information and the speed at which it can be exchanged have increased dramatically. Rapid and robust information flow saves time and money. It transforms organizations because it eliminates paper-based functions, flattens organizational layers, and integrates global operations.

With the availability of greater bandwidth at lower costs, the cost of computing will decrease dramatically. This will bring about tremendous changes in the way the world operates—from the speed at which the economy functions and the ways in which the economy is configured, to how profits are made and lost. It will change how we educate, govern, and live our daily lives.

Most of the economy is configured based on the cost of interactions and the cost of transactions. In other words, the cost that a customer pays to buy something is a function of the transaction cost, and the speed at which the interactions occur and how efficiently they occur. With the information revolution in general and the Internet in particular, all of those things are put into a big blender at high speed and turned into something completely different.

I've mentioned before that the value of inventory is being replaced by the value of information. Physical assets are being traded for intellectual assets. Any small business can equip itself with PCs connected to the Internet and have the tools of a large business at its disposal. Closed business systems are giving way to collaborative relationships, and businesses are far more dependent on one another than ever before.

It used to be that proprietary technologies, priced at a premium, provided the main source of competitive advantage. But as the information industry continues to mature and the companies in it become more fully developed, I believe that product differentiation, while still important, will become much harder to achieve. It will give way to *process* innovation as the fundamental source of competitive advantage.

And with the advent of the Internet, innovation won't be measured in minor increments. The Internet is blurring traditional boundaries between supplier and manufacturer, and manufacturer and customer. This shrinks time and distance to a degree never before possible. And while many have focused on online commerce, I believe the use of the Internet as a sales channel represents only a fraction of the Internet's value to business. The real potential of the Internet lies in its ability to transform relationships within the traditional supplier-vendor-customer chain.

Those businesses that don't embrace these changes will end up
roadkill on the information superhighway.

SEIZE THE OPPORTUNITIES AFFORDED BY
A LEVEL PLAYING FIELD

One of the most phenomenal developments related to the Internet is
how it levels the playing field. The benefits and effects aren't limited
to large businesses, or businesses that make a certain profit. Because
the Internet doesn't discriminate, there are incredible opportunities
for small businesses to usurp market share from industry leaders.

I think we're going to see a whole new wave of rapid industry transition—unlike the slow transition of, say, transportation, in which it
took many years to go from rail to air travel. In this transition, you will
see traditionally structured companies being seriously challenged by
new, smaller, more efficient entrants—right away. The logical extension of the Internet's cost efficiencies means that market share will flow
to the most efficient companies, not the largest or the richest—companies that can deliver the greatest value to their customers will earn a
higher profit while requiring far fewer assets. The productivity of their
capital will be significantly improved over the traditional model
because they will have replaced physical assets with information assets.

Because that information will be moving at super-high rates of
speed, they will have a much simpler and more efficient system.
There will be no question of "Did we forecast correctly? Did we put
our physical assets (stores and inventory)—essentially, did we place
our bets—in the right places?" As a result, these businesses will be far
more scaleable than traditional companies—especially if they enter
large markets—and they will be able to grow at very high rates for
very extended periods of time.

It won't happen in all product categories at once, but it will
happen. And no one can know exactly what the world will look like

when this all shakes out. But you can look at both Dell and Amazon.com for a preview. By embracing the Internet early and aggressively, both companies have charged the competitive landscape of our industries with a whole new cost structure and level of efficiency. Once these new levels become the norm rather than the exception, competitive value will be based on service and personalization, convenience, and ease of interaction.

Companies that master this will experience much faster growth than their industry norms, with consistent year-to-year sales and profit increases of at least 30 percent. That's hypergrowth—and yes, I do believe you can sustain it in the connected economy.

GO FOR HYPERGROWTH

Conventional wisdom dictates that hypergrowth can't be sustained over a long period of time. Why? Traditionally, the feeling is that the company is either out of control or that the inevitable rhythm of product life cycles will take its toll and growth will slow.

Again, I say conventional wisdom is wrong. At Dell, we have been living with this level of growth—and more—for fifteen years. By integrating virtually with both our customers and our suppliers, we have been able to achieve a highly scaleable business, and continue to grow at over twice the industry rate. Now we're seeing this phenomenon happen with more and more companies. Not surprisingly, many of them are new companies in Internet-based industries, or are companies that have embraced the Internet as a core part of business strategy.

So just how does a company like Dell sustain its growth? And how can a company like yours experience hypergrowth?

Your economic ability must be influenced by a superior product or service. And you must understand the fundamental economics unique to your industry and where the opportunities exist.

In our case, we created what we believe is the smartest way to buy and own a PC. We also systematically add new businesses that are closely related and build on one another's momentum. The desktop business, for example, is a great business but you can assume that as a company succeeds, the growth rate of that particular business will slow to approximate the industry. Desktops by themselves, in other words, aren't enough to sustain momentum over a long period of time. However, by successfully adding on a series of businesses—be they products (like servers and workstations), services (like leasing, DellPlus, and asset management), or geographies (like China and South America)—we've been able to keep our growth rate above 40 percent over the past seven years.

Of course, we had to build and scale our infrastructure to keep pace with our growth; balancing the need for supporting infrastructure without building infrastructure too far ahead of growth is one of the more difficult and ongoing challenges any hypergrowth company will face.

But a hypergrowth company's relative lack of a past—of sacred strategies, or long-established practices and procedures—means that it will have a better chance to improvise as it goes. Hypergrowth companies are quintessential learn-by-doing organizations. Their survival depends on swift adaptation. Because resources and people are stretched, they most likely don't have excessive formal or overly structured systems in place. The key is to have enough structure in place that growth is not out of control—but not so much that the structure impedes your ability to adapt quickly.

If a young growth company sufficiently believes in its future, it will invest in the management skills and controls that can sustain high performance over many decades. And while hypergrowth may not be sustainable forever—as nothing lasts that long, and many factors can and will intervene—it is the best rehearsal for decades of impressive and reliably managed growth.

INTEGRATE VIRTUALLY

The Internet is both turbocharging the way many companies do business and expediting the shift from the traditional business model of vertical integration to one of virtual integration. By creating information partnerships with customers and suppliers, Dell has obtained the benefits of tightly coordinated supply chain management that have normally been associated with vertically integrated companies. At the same time, we have been able to continue to focus on our core competencies to maintain the speed and flexibility required to compete in the Information Age. This is what we mean by virtual integration, which is centered on information assets, compared to vertical integration, which relies on the acquisition of physical assets.

For Dell, the concept behind virtual integration is a natural evolution of our direct business model. Our company was founded on the simple premise that by selling personal computer systems directly to customers, Dell could quickly understand their needs and provide the most effective computing solutions to meet those needs. Because we started the company with so little capital, we had to define our value-add very narrowly. Instead of trying to be excellent at making all the pieces and parts that went into the finished product, we partnered for those capital-intensive services with suppliers—and focused on delivering customer-directed solutions.

The ultimate goal of virtual integration for us is improving the total customer experience. Our company has always been focused on the customer, but we believe we can do even better. By developing a kind of "empathetic viewpoint" we try to see things exactly as our customers do and, in turn, can begin to dramatically improve the customer experience. It's not enough to have the best service in the computer industry; we want to be ranked with the premier service companies of the world, like Nordstrom and FedEx. Accordingly, we look to learn from them, constantly asking questions such as "How easy is it for a customer to track a package electronically through FedEx?" Or "How friendly is the Nordstrom experience?" We're looking to compete not just with computer companies but with the companies that are best at providing a great experience to their customers.

No one company can succeed by itself. We need help from our partners—the Intels, the Microsofts, the logistics companies, the field service organizations, and the disk drive and CRT manufacturers, as well as all our people, from frontline operations in sales, service, and manufacturing to human resources, finance, and all the other groups that back them up. Virtual integration is essential to the process of delivering the optimal customer experience, as it requires a truly integrated effort among all the companies with which we work.

LINK YOUR WORLD, ELECTRONICALLY

The Internet provides the ultimate extension of a network of users; it links the whole world electronically.

Gone are the days of stocking your store in the hope that you're close to predicting how much and what your customers will want. The ease and efficiency of buying over the Internet breaks down these barriers, providing a way to measure how much inventory is left, what your cost structure is, and where your profit margins fall.

Manufacturers can no longer afford to treat suppliers like vendors from whom every last ounce of cost-saving can be wrung. Nor can we treat customers simply like a market for products and services at the best possible price. Instead, we need to treat both suppliers and customers like partners and collaborators—together looking for ways to improve efficiency and value across the *entire* spectrum of the value chain, not just in our respective businesses. In this way, we can create deeper and more enduring relationships that result in *shared* efficiencies, far greater loyalty, and enhanced long-term value for all concerned.

At Dell, we're trying to build an organization where we can

achieve integration across all functions. Integration with our customers, with our people, and with our suppliers are each good in and of themselves. The model really cranks, however, when you integrate all three. That's the ultimate power and the promise of dealing direct, and it's powered by the Internet. To succeed, you must position yourself to take advantage of the Internet and to build information partnerships with your suppliers and customers. If you don't, you won't survive. If you do, you will have the potential to be a part of a fundamental change in global competition and redefine the value you provide to your customers and shareholders.

The results will be nothing short of revolutionary.

These are the strategies that have led, in large part, to our success. Building on them is what will ensure success in the connected economy, as much for your business as for ours:

◆ Expect change—and plan for it. Rather than seeing it as a potential threat or problem, welcome it as an opportunity. Encourage your people to seek out the indicators of change in your particular industry. Remember: There's no risk in preserving the status quo, but there's no profit, either.

◆ Exploit the Internet. The Internet is the most effective and pervasive change agent in this connected economy. Regardless of your industry, you cannot afford to continue to do "business as usual." Use the Internet to break down traditional boundaries—if you're a large corporation, it can help you connect more directly with your people, customers, and suppliers; it can enable you to work faster and become more adept at riding the waves of change. If you're a small business, it evens the score between you and the big guys by reducing the cost of interactions and transactions and opening new avenues of communication and competition.

◆ Reorient your priorities. Price is not the prevailing factor in the connected economy; as the Internet levels the competitive playing field, competitive value is more apt to be found in execution. Stress personalization, convenience, and ease of interaction for your customers.

◆ Go for growth—deliberately. Becoming a hypergrowth company requires equal parts improvisation and planning. You can attain *and* sustain high levels of growth in the connected economy.

◆ Integrate your business—virtually. Search for ways to partner virtually in an effort to eliminate steps, enhance efficiencies, and provide a better total customer experience. Strive to be the best in the world, not just the best in your business.

IN CONCLUSION

DELL HAS, THUS FAR, ENJOYED A GREAT deal of success. I'd like to think of it as a great start. Our stock is up more than 79,000 percent over the last ten years. In that same time, we've grown from a $389 million company to a $30 billion company.

So, naturally, people ask me when Dell will slow down or when the PC market will become saturated.

I genuinely believe that we are a part of what's rapidly becoming the largest industry in the world—and that this is only the beginning. The usage rate and penetration rate for PCs is still quite low compared to the size of the world's population. Considering how products like the television or calculator or even the telephone have evolved over time and infiltrated millions of businesses and billions of households, I believe that the same will happen over time with PCs. Accordingly, the market for personal computers and related products and services will experience tremendous growth and much deeper penetration rates in the global economy over the next ten or twenty years.

I know that no company can continue to grow at greater than 50 percent per year forever. However, I also believe that Dell has incredible opportunities to grow faster than our industry for a long time to come.

Why?

Our company still has only 11 percent market share. If we had 50 percent market share—like Coca-Cola—I might be a little more concerned about our growth slowing to the industry rate. And even though we're number one in some markets, 11 percent doesn't nearly satisfy the opportunities that are available to us as we continue to add new geographies, new products, new customer segments, new services, and, above all, a better customer experience. Even our most mature businesses are still growing significantly faster than industry.

We also have a structural economic advantage and a ton of opportunities yet to exploit. Consider the businesses we could add. Think products, and you've got desktops, notebooks, servers, storage, and more. Think geographies, and you've got the United States, Europe, Japan, Asia, and South America. Think strategies that have driven growth: building to order, segmentation, the Internet, targeting a customer of one.

I believe we have the right business model for the Internet age. We have a significant lead in dealing direct with customers and suppliers, which we believe will prove even more invaluable as the market shifts from indirect to direct distribution, and our competitors clamor to catch up. Perhaps most important of all, we have created a partnership of trust and communication among our most significant allies: our people, our customers, and our suppliers. Together we face the future with a healthy sense of adventure, a love of learning, and a willingness to embrace change in an ever-changing industry.

No, there's no such thing as a company that executes perfectly forever. But the real key to our success comes from within. It comes from knowing our strengths and being open to experimentation. It comes from the determination to learn from our mistakes and look for ways to continually improve. It comes from being willing to challenge conventional wisdom and having the courage to follow our convictions. It comes from an innate fascination with eliminating unnecessary steps

These are the true roots of strategies that should continue to help us—and you—revolutionize our industries for a long time to come.

www.dell.com www.dell.com www.dell.com www.dell.com **www.dell.com** www.d

INDEX

www.dell.com www.dell.com www.dell.com www.dell.com **www.dell.com** www.d

ABOUT THE AUTHOR

MICHAEL S. DELL IS CHAIRMAN AND chief executive officer of Dell Computer Corporation, the leading direct computer company and one of the fastest-growing computer systems companies in the world. He founded the company in 1984 with $1,000 and an unprecedented idea in the personal computer industry: bypass the middleman and sell custom-built PCs directly to end-users. Using this innovative direct-marketing approach, Dell Computer Corporation has established itself as one of the top two vendors of personal computers worldwide. Its corporate customers include most of the companies on the Fortune 500 list of America's largest companies. With the addition of Dell Computer Corporation to this list several years ago, Mr. Dell became the youngest CEO of a company ever to earn a ranking on the Fortune 500. Fortune now ranks Dell Computer the fourth most admired company in the United States and the ninth wordwide.

Michael Dell has been honored many times for his visionary leadership, earning the titles "Entrepreneur of the Year" from *Inc.* magazine, "Man of the Year" by *PC* magazine, and "CEO of the Year" by *Financial World* magazine, among many others. In 1997, 1998 and 1999, he was included in *Business Week*'s list of "The Top 25 Managers of the Year." He is a member of the Board of Directors of the United States Chamber of Commerce and the Computerworld/Smithsonian Awards.